T0267006

"As one of so many who prayed for Greg Mundis during his life-and-death ordeal, I witnessed the enduring faith of a family who never stopped believing he would fully recover against all odds. *Patient #1* will encourage readers to hold on to hope sourced in God, even in life's darkest hours."

John Ashcroft
Former Attorney General of the United States

"Ever wonder how people live 'through' life crises and if there is a light at the end of the tunnel? Packed with authentic, heartwarming stories, I am recommending this book as a required 'reading assignment' to all of my patients and families who are going through a medical crisis of any sort."

Kore Liow, M.D.
Practicing neurologist, Hawaii Pacific Neuroscience

"Reality comes at you quickly during the darkest moments of your life. *Unexpected* and *overwhelming* are two words that would express what Greg, Sandie, and their family were facing in the spring of 2020. Yet in the midst of the chaos they found incredible love, strength, and healing. So grateful that they are sharing their journey of hope and life with the world."

Mark Lehmann
Lead Pastor, Cornerstone Church

"This book reminds us that miracles still take place! Written in a narrative style, Greg and Sandie captivate their audience with their vulnerability as they graciously chronicle their own tumultuous journey. Their story will inspire you and resuscitate the hope you need when walking through moments of crisis."

Melissa Alfaro, Ph.D.
Educator and Author

"The reality of COVID-19 was still somewhat of a mystery to me until my friend Greg Mundis made its severity abundantly clear. The Mundis family became the early face of the pandemic to many of us who love and respect this leadership family so dearly. Greg's courageous battle with this devastating virus will remind you of God's faithfulness, even in the darkest seasons of this life. I highly recommend this book!"

Erik Cooper
President, The Stone Stable

"Greg Mundis is a respected leader, colleague, and friend. For many, he was also the sobering introduction to the reality and devastation of COVID-19. This is the riveting story of a courageous man and his family who dared to hope and pray for his recovery (again and again!), always in the face of death. Greg Mundis' COVID journey defied all odds. What an inspiring reminder to all who read that the impossible is still possible with God."

Dr. Beth Grant
Executive Director, Project Rescue

"A powerful and captivating story of the struggle to find confident hope in the throes of chaos and uncertainty. Their honest account reveals the truth we all need in difficult, fearful times: authentic peace is only possible when we merge complete trust in God with genuine surrender to His will."

Joseph Walter
Executive Director and Vice President of a charitable foundation

"To anyone needing a fresh glimpse of hope, and belief that miracles do still happen, this is the book for you. From the first page, I was captured by the raw emotions of fear and uncertainty, yet hope against all odds that love was going to win and things would turn out okay. Do yourself a favor: read this book and breathe a deep breath of fresh air."

Scott Marcum
Real Estate Investment Asset Manager

"This book will encourage and strengthen anyone that is going through or will go through dark days in their life!"

Jack E. Thurman
Former Managing Partner of Baird, Kurtz & Dobson LLP

PATIENT

embracing *Hope*
in times of despair

Sandra & Greg Mundis
with Anneliese Dalaba

HIGHERLIFE
PUBLISHING & MARKETING

Published by HigherLife Development Services Inc.
PO Box 623307
Oviedo, Florida 32762
www.ahigherlife.com

ISBN: 978-1-958211-43-4 (Hardback)
978-1-958211-44-1 (Paperback)
978-1-958211-45-8 (ebook)

Printed in the United States of America.

10 9 8 7 6 5 4 3 2 1

TABLE OF CONTENTS

Foreword ix

Random 1

Against All Odds 15

Battle Rages 27

Rubber Band 55

#rallyhope...77

Wake Up...105

Welcome Home 135

Epilogue 155

Acknowledgments...171

WHEN THE BOSNIA-HERZEGOVINA WAR ended, Greg Mundis and I traveled to the battered country. Despite UN peacekeeping forces, the city of Mostar was haunted by the horrors of war: buildings leveled by mortar shells; community parks converted to graveyards; transportation systems, power grids, and water sources disrupted; and the homeless perched on fractured sidewalks.

After two days touring the rubble and listening to citizens relive their nightmare, I found myself emotionally empty. I had seen enough death and destruction for one trip. I just wanted to retreat to my room and cry myself to sleep. Instead, that night I piled into a car with Greg and our co-worker, Randy Hurst, to speak to a gathering of Muslims, Catholics, and Protestants. The war between them was left outside the walls of the meeting hall and they gathered together to find faith, hope, and love from God.

When we arrived, more than two hundred people were wedged into a small room, singing enthusiastically. The crowd applauded as Greg was introduced. He took the microphone and, with the help of an interpreter, launched into a spirited message. He said, "God is with you and so are your brothers and sisters around the world. God will never leave you nor forsake you."

From the back of the room, I watched as men and women wiped tears and nodded in agreement. With each word, their hope was being restored—and so was mine. With his towering voice, Greg urged the crowd to trust God in every situation. "When we face hardship," he said, "we can turn to the Lord for help and know that He hears and answers prayer."

That night in Mostar is etched in my memory. Greg was a portrait of strength, courage, and compassion for people who had suffered great loss. That is one reason why, in March 2020, it was difficult for me to comprehend that he was now lying unconscious in a hospital bed, having contracted the coronavirus. (He was the first patient with the virus to be vented and placed in ICU at Mercy Hospital in Springfield, Missouri.)

As the hours passed and Greg's condition declined, doctors informed his wife, Sandie, and two grown children that there was little hope of recovery. Despite a bleak prognosis, dedicated doctors and nurses continued to work tirelessly while family and friends around the globe prayed relentlessly.

Patient #1 is the gripping story of Greg's journey from death's door to wholeness. It is also the story of a wife, children, and grandchildren who never lost hope. They refused to give up, believing Greg would one day walk out of that hospital and return to his post. The Mundises had learned a long time ago to trust God in every situation.

The rest of the story will stir your emotions and shower you with hope. Regardless of your circumstances or the size of miracle you need, *Patient #1* is a reminder that God is with you and He still does the impossible.

Read on and discover the power of faith and hope in your own life.

Hal Donaldson
President, Convoy of Hope

"He causes his sun to rise on the evil and the good,

And sends rain on the righteous and the unrighteous."

Matthew 5:45 NIV

CHAPTER 1

Random

WHEN WOULD THIS FEVER break? Every time a wave of chills hit, I shook so uncontrollably that my teeth rattled. It hurt to move, and it hurt to sit still. I pulled the blankets higher as I stared at sterile, bare walls and attempted to inhale a deep breath. The tightness in my chest made it difficult.

The nurse call button lay beside my aching fingers. No one had been in to check on me in quite a while. Had they received my COVID test results yet? Even though by all indications I had contracted the virus from my husband, Greg, verification would bring closure to the uncertainty.

The doctors' and nurses' routine every time they entered and exited my room seemed like something from another planet. Always in hazmat suits, their triple-masked head gear made for unclear speech when they spoke. I sensed their obvious fear as they peered through thick masks to examine me. Before the staff departed, the squeaky sounds of glove removal were accompanied by sounds of masks and entire body coverings torn off and tossed into the trash container. Then they scurried to the door as fast as possible, without a backward glance. It made me feel unclean, perhaps like the lepers felt in biblical times.

I turned my head away from the door and gazed out the window. Only the sky was visible. It looked as bleak as my dreary room. Did other people's lives come to a complete standstill as mine had in just one week?

Everything screamed of isolation. Visitors were not permitted entry to my quarantine room—not even our son, Greg Jr., who is a surgeon in San Diego, California, but currently staying in a hotel across from this hospital. Friends and family stayed in touch through texts, FaceTime, emails, and phone calls. In this forced separation, it was a blessing that modern technology allowed our daughter, Hollie, and her family to stay in almost constant contact from their home in Israel.

I tried to encourage myself that we would make it through somehow. If only I had answers to the haunting questions that filled my mind. Hope and doubt combatted each other for dominance. Would I ever see my husband again? Would I be able to say goodbye if he passed away? Would I also end up in ICU on a ventilator? Would we die together?

Tears poured over my feverish cheeks. I felt confined. There were no hugs to comfort and no hands to hold. Just this barren room with a single bed, a sink, and a trash can with discarded gloves, masks, and gowns that had protected those who had dared to touch me . . . and there was a window.

I closed my tired eyes to pray and turned my thoughts toward my Savior and Best Friend. I could count on Him. He had brought us through many crises in the past, so I determined to trust Him with this new frightening enigma we found ourselves in. Finally relaxing, a song from my childhood filtered into my mind: *He's all I need. He's all I need. Jesus is all I need.*

As I sang the simple lyrics in a soft, strained voice, peace and hope swept over me. The empty, cold room filled with Jesus's all-encompassing presence, and I cried to Him like so many times before. Again, I shared with Him my deepest and most troubling fears, and I knew He heard me.

I reached for my Bible on the hospital bed table and opened to Psalm 91 where I had read that morning. My eyes fell on the second verse: "He is my refuge and my fortress, my God, in whom I trust."

The familiar words soothed. I had repeatedly experienced their truth in my life, especially this past week. And now, they once again breathed hope and assurance into my mind and heart. *In you, Lord, I will take refuge.*

My head rested on the pillow as I whispered over and over, "In you, Lord, I will take refuge. You are my fortress."

I must have fallen asleep. The ringing of my cell phone woke me. Greg Jr.'s familiar voice spoke. "Mom, I have to go get some food. If you can make it to the window, you'll see me waving at you."

Of course I wanted to see my son, even if it was from a distance. Pushing the covers aside, I ignored the pain and slowly lowered my feet to the floor. Carefully, I made my way to the window while holding onto the IV pole. Way off in the distance, in a diagonal direction from the seventh floor, past the entrance of the hospital and across the street to the hotel on the next block, I recognized my car, which I had thoroughly sanitized for our son's use. Next to it stood Greg Jr. with his arm raised. It was impossible to see him clearly, but that didn't matter. Fixing my eyes on my son, I waved and waved.

I continued watching until he drove off and the taillights were out of view. As I hobbled back to my bed and climbed in, the obvious reminders of a world turned upside down dominated like a plague. The cold wave of isolation rose to its peak again. How long would we all live separated from each other due to the required quarantine? The virus was a mystery, and fear tried, with fierce determination, to grip my heart as I contemplated our new reality.

It boggled my mind how much had changed in just one week.

Seven days prior was March 12, 2020. I will never forget that day—it was a Thursday. I had taken the spouses of my husband's colleagues to see a historical performance on stage in a neighboring city. We enjoyed a typical Ozark lunch with lots of laughter and conversation. No one wore masks or talked about social distancing. It was unheard of. As I looked back now, life seemed so simple a week ago.

While at the show with my guests, I received a text from my husband. *Sandie, I don't feel well.*

He was in the middle of a board meeting. I immediately responded, *What's wrong?*

Feels like the flu.

Oh, no. This wasn't a good time to get sick, especially since we still had to attend the closing dinner that evening for our colleagues and their spouses. It was important for our executive team to close out this celebratory week with this dinner. Greg is the Director of Assemblies of God World Missions (AGWM), and these were people on our mission's board who came from all over the USA only two times a year for our semiannual board meetings.

Later that afternoon I texted Greg asking how he was doing.

I feel awful. My body aches all over and I have a sore throat. I think I might have to cancel going to the dinner tonight. I don't want to get others sick.

What? Greg would never want to miss this dinner. It was completely out of character for him. He must feel terrible.

That evening at home, Greg picked at his simple meal. He looked exhausted and his body aches continued, along with a runny nose and sore throat, so he went to bed early, insisting it was just a cold of some sort. I had my doubts. He mentioned that his ankles, knees, and even his wrists hurt. Maybe he had a new kind of respiratory virus affecting his whole body. I worried because Greg had an allergy to the flu vaccine and had not yet gone to our primary care doctor for the special vaccine through the nose. What if he was unprotected from this peculiar influenza?

When Greg awoke the next day, he had a fever. At least he would be going to the clinic that morning. Without a doubt, they would identify whatever bug he may have picked up. Greg was sure a few prescribed medicines would take care of it.

"You have a sinus infection," the physician's assistant informed him. "I'll send a script in for antibiotics. You'll be feeling much better in a few days."

What a relief! We had dealt with sinus infections before. We just needed to give this time. I sympathized with Greg since I also experienced sinus infections due to asthma. But why the body aches? That seemed odd to me. Regardless, I set my battle plan in motion. I would make him some tea and then let him rest. After all, as my mom often said, sleep was the best remedy when you're sick.

While Greg napped, I called our son. I wanted his professional input from a physician's point of view. Greg Jr. wondered if it could be the new virus, COVID-19. He knew his dad had entertained colleagues from Europe the previous week, and the virus was becoming prevalent in those countries. I doubted it was that particular virus. It seemed too far-fetched.

Later that afternoon, our son-in-law, Jason, came to see us. He was attending meetings in Springfield and had flown in all the way from Israel where he served with our daughter, Hollie, and our four grandchildren. We had been in touch yesterday, but when Greg got sick, we thought it best for him to stay elsewhere in case Greg was contagious. However, he came by to say hi, and he brought us toilet paper and paper towels, which were becoming scarce in the United States since the eleventh of March—two days ago—when the World Health Organization declared the novel coronavirus a *global pandemic*.[1] It seemed

---

1   Domenico Cucinotta & Maurizio Vanelli, "WHO Declares CO-VID-19 a Pandemic," *Acta Biomed.* 91, no. 1 (March 19, 2020); 157-160. doi: 10.23750/abm.v91i1.9397

outrageous how quickly people were filled with fear and buying up every basic necessity they could find. Jason explained that he had gone all over town before he finally found a package of toilet paper on a store shelf. How strange—of all places, he tracked down a few rolls at a hardware store.

Jason placed his armload of supplies on the table and went to greet Greg, who sat in his recliner. Noticing that his father-in-law could barely focus and seemed to struggle to say hello, Jason looked at me in grave concern. Unable to carry on a conversation, he joined me in another room and shared his disquieting thoughts. He'd never seen Greg like this. He wondered if it was COVID-19.

I still thought it highly unlikely—especially not here in Springfield, Missouri. However, Jason had now expressed the same concerns as Greg Jr.

Later, Hollie told me Jason had texted her immediately upon leaving our house, telling her, "Your dad is really, really sick. I think it's COVID."

On Saturday, per the recommendation of our primary care doctor, Greg was tested for various flus, but the results were all negative. However, as the day progressed, his symptoms worsened. He became weak and lethargic, and his body aches intensified. To me, this seemed like more than a sinus infection.

I began reading all I could find about this aggressive new virus. As I searched the internet, alarming headlines painted a grim picture.

Trump declares state of emergency over coronavirus.[2]

---

2   "A Timeline of COVID-19 Developments in 2020," AJMC, accessed

New York state reports first two fatalities.[3]

As many as 200,000 to 1.7 million people could die from COVID-19 in the United States alone.[4]

I had to discover what the symptoms of this virus were. As I searched, I learned the three symptoms to look for were *fever, cough,* and *shortness of breath*. It relieved me to realize that Greg only had one of the three symptoms, a fever. Perhaps it wasn't COVID.

> **I had to discover what the symptoms of this virus were. I learned the three symptoms to look for were fever, cough, and shortness of breath.**

That evening, we received news that the three colleagues from Europe had tested positive for COVID-19. A chill ran down my spine. Could this really be what we were dealing with after all?

I wanted to get Greg into the emergency room, but they weren't accepting walk-ins. What was going on? I tried to contact various places to receive some medical attention over the weekend, but no one returned my calls. My frustration increased with every failed attempt.

In case Greg had COVID, our son instructed me not to sleep in the same room with Greg since the virus was highly

December 15, 2022, https://www.ajmc.com/view/a-timeline-of-covid19-developments-in-2020.

3   ABC News, World News Tonight, WLAJ53, S11 E73, Saturday, March 14, 2020, NR|03.14.20|20:31|CC

4   Joshua Cohen, "Accuracy Of Estimate Of 100,000 To 240,000 Covid-19 Deaths Hinges On Key Assumptions," *Forbes*, accessed December 15, 2022, https://www.forbes.com/sites/joshuacohen/2020/04/02/accuracy-of-estimate-of-100000-to-240000-covid-19-deaths-hinges-on-key-assumptions/?sh=22069308144e

contagious. The medical reports stated that anyone with a compromised immune system could become much sicker with this virus than people without preexisting conditions. That list included people with asthma and diabetes, both of which I have. But I didn't want to be far away, so I chose to sleep on the couch in the family room with the bedroom door open so I could hear him if he called out to me or developed shortness of breath.

As I lay on the couch under the covers, only a few feet away from Greg, I could hear his congestion. He moaned from time to time. I racked my brain trying to think of what else I could do. I checked on him from the bedroom doorway throughout the night.

Since I couldn't sleep with my increasing concern, I prayed fervently on and off throughout the night. The verse in James 1:5 came to mind: "If any of you lacks wisdom, you should ask God, who gives generously to all without finding fault, and it will be given to you." So that's what I did. I needed to hear from the Lord. At some point while I prayed, I fell asleep.

I awoke before my husband on Sunday, so I picked up my smartphone to check the latest news. *There are 1,629 total U.S. cases of COVID-19 and 41 deaths as of Friday, March 13. Due to lack of early testing, this is almost definitely an undercount.*

The more I read and heard about COVID, the more I suspected Greg really had become infected with this virus. But how could I confirm it? Between the news reports and Greg's condition, it was impossible not to feel anxious.

When Greg didn't show any signs of improvement after he awoke, and his fever had risen, I became desperate.

Remembering my plea for wisdom, I prayed that the Lord would help me reach someone in our area. I called the State of Missouri Center of Disease Control (CDC) and talked to a registered nurse. I explained my husband's symptoms and about the internationals he'd spent time with and the fact that they had tested positive for COVID. I left nothing out.

The nurse listened intently and asked questions. She doubted Greg had COVID-19. He didn't have all three of the main symptoms since he didn't have a cough or shortness of breath—just a fever. She suggested I *not* take him to the hospital. Instead, she encouraged me to continue watching Greg until Monday morning, and then try to contact our primary care doctor to discuss what we could do at that point.

I felt helpless. Why was Greg getting worse? Did he have to have all the symptoms to have COVID? He was so sick and there was nothing I could do to help him except to pray.

Conversations between Hollie, Greg Jr., and his wife, Lesley, occupied the whole day. They wanted to check on their dad and became more concerned as the day progressed. Jason was on his way back to Israel and would text or call during his layovers. Close friends and family voiced their concerns, but since there was no definitive diagnosis, we said Greg was still sick and please pray. Nothing was made public or put on social media for two reasons—I wasn't in a frame of mind to formulate statements, and I didn't want to disseminate false information without a confirmed diagnosis. However, prayer in a small group had already begun around the clock.

By Monday morning, Greg was growing more listless. I frantically called the primary care doctor's office at seven and left a message on their after-hours answering service. "Please call me. This is urgent." Then I described my husband's symptoms.

My phone rang at around eight o'clock. The primary care doctor's name flashed on the screen, and I jumped to answer it. Finally, we'll get some answers.

The doctor requested a COVID test. She scheduled it at eleven that morning and explained we'd have to drive to a particular park where a tent was set up, stay in the car, and someone would come up to the window and swab Greg's nose.

I drove Greg through a rainstorm to the outdoor testing site. On the way, Greg Jr. called, and after reviewing his dad's worsening condition, he suspected lack of oxygen was causing his lethargy. He asked if we owned an oximeter so I could measure Greg's heartbeat and oxygen level. I told him we didn't. Our son feared his dad's oxygen level was plummeting, and insisted I take him to the hospital emergency room.

After the nasal test was completed, the nurse informed us that we would receive the results in about four days. On our drive home, our doctor called. "I've already got an ambulance coming. Greg will be taken to the hospital. It doesn't sound good. No matter what his symptoms are, they don't sound right to me either."

It was early afternoon when the ambulance arrived. The EMTs came to the door in full hazmat gear. My eyes widened as I stared in bewilderment. This kind of stuff only happened in movies. I let them in, of course, and they rushed to Greg, touching him as little as possible.

When I moved toward them, one of the men held out a hand. "Stop! Don't come near us, and don't come near your husband either."

I stared as they continued working. They didn't want me near *Greg*? Who did they think had been caring for him all weekend?

After one of the EMTs measured Greg's oxygen level, I heard him tell his colleague, "We need to get him on oxygen immediately. He's only measuring 60 percent!"

I remembered Greg Jr. had suspected his dad's lethargy was due to insufficient oxygen. Anything below 90 percent indicated an emergency. My heart pounded with fear. This was all so new to me.

Once Greg was on the gurney, they began rolling him toward the front door. As he passed me, our gazes met. Greg's eyes seemed dazed and glazed over, while filled with despondency, questions, and confusion. After forty-nine years of marriage, I had learned to read him well even without words. He wondered if he'd ever see me again. I swallowed back tears, refusing to make it harder for him. Oh, how I longed to touch him, to hold his hand and reassure him, but the hurried steps of the EMTs rolled him to the ambulance.

From ten feet away, I raised my voice. "Don't worry, Honey. I'll meet you at the hospital. They'll take good care of you. I love you. See you there."

The EMTs nixed that idea. "You aren't allowed anywhere *near* the hospital. Until we know this isn't COVID, you must quarantine. Don't leave your house and don't allow anyone to enter. Someone from the Health Department will call you. You should hear from the hospital in about two hours."

> **"Stop! Don't come near us, and don't come near your husband either."**

I watched in stunned silence as they jumped into the ambulance and backed out of the driveway. They rode off with my husband, the man I loved beyond measure—the other half of myself. When the ambulance pulled away, a chunk of my heart went with them. Greg was in the hands of strangers now. Would they fight for his life the way I would? I had to trust them. My husband was completely at their mercy, dependent on people we had never seen and knew nothing about.

Even when I could no longer see the ambulance, my ears continued to follow the sounds of the loud sirens that resonated the seriousness of our perplexing crisis.

"I AM COUNTING ON THE
LORD;
YES, I AM COUNTING ON HIM.
I HAVE PUT MY HOPE IN HIS
WORD."

PSALM 130:5 NLT

CHAPTER TWO

Against All Odds

AFTER THE AMBULANCE PULLED away, I waited until the piercing sound of the siren faded, then turned and entered the house. I shut the door and stared in a daze. What had just happened?

I clenched my fists. Even though the EMTs made it clear it was the contagiousness of COVID-19 that brought about the new hospital restrictions, I found it unbelievable that they wouldn't let me follow Greg to the hospital in our car. I couldn't wrap my mind around how fast life had changed. It all seemed unreal, like I was living a nightmare.

The look in Greg's eyes and the EMTs' hurried actions haunted me. Fear raised its ugly head. I collapsed on the couch, crying, "Lord, help me navigate these next steps. Show me what I'm supposed to do!"

After the tears subsided, I pulled myself together. Inhaling deeply, I realized there was much for which to be thankful amid this frightening crisis. Greg was now in a place where a skilled medical team would help him, even if I couldn't be there with him. Certainly, they would know how to assist him toward full recovery.

I called my children to apprise them of the situation, explaining that the EMTs had taken Greg's blood oxygen level, and it was 60 percent—a horrible reading. Then I explained that I wasn't allowed to follow him to the hospital but had to quarantine instead. I couldn't leave the house, and no one could come inside. The EMTs said someone from the emergency room would call in about two hours, and I would also hear from County Health Services sometime that day.

At that point, Greg Jr. began a family text that included Lesley, Hollie, Jason, and me. This allowed us to share information all at one time.

The next few hours were agonizing as I waited for a phone call from the hospital. I talked with our kids off and on, and we prayed together. I spoke with our executive missions administrator, Kevin, about Greg being admitted to the hospital, and he shared this information with the expanded leadership team so they could begin praying. Since we didn't yet know Greg's diagnosis, we didn't want to share specifics on social media.

Health Services called, and we spoke for about a half hour. They asked numerous questions:

- *When did Greg's symptoms begin?*
- *What were his symptoms?*
- *Why was an ambulance called?*
- *When did he get his COVID-19 test?*
- *Starting two days before his symptoms began, with whom had he been in contact? They needed the name of each person.*

Since I didn't have the information for their last request, I referred the question to Kevin, who would be able to list the many people in the office and anyone else with whom Greg had come in contact. When they asked if I knew from whom Greg might have contracted the disease, I mentioned the colleagues from Europe. I also informed her that today we heard that our friend, Ron, who was an AGWM Regional Director, was very sick with some of the same symptoms. He had also been in the meetings with the colleagues from Europe.

They reiterated that I had to quarantine alone in my house, allowing no one else inside. I was not to go out for any reason, so I should either arrange to have someone deliver food or order directly from a store. No delivery person may enter the house. I had a lot of adjusting to do in this new world, whether I wanted to or not.

After two more hours passed and I still hadn't heard any news from the hospital about Greg, I became antsy and decided to call Greg's cell phone. It was worth a try. What could it hurt? I had made sure to pack his phone in his bag along with his hearing aids, eyeglass case, and a few additional items. I handed it all to the EMTs before they transported him to the ambulance. After a few rings, I debated if I should hang up. To my surprise, a nurse answered Greg's phone and allowed him to talk to me.

We only spoke for thirty seconds. His voice was frail and breathy, and he talked in short phrases. He said he was in the emergency room, in bad shape, had bad lungs, and they would be admitting him. He finished with, "Please don't worry. Hollie and Greg will take care of everything. They're going to take care of you. I love you."

I couldn't believe his main concern was about me when he was the one so sick.

My heart sank. I was on the brink of despair as he struggled for each breath. Gathering every ounce of strength, I reassured him that I would be okay and not to worry about me. He should focus on following his doctors' orders so he could get well.

At about 3:15 p.m., the ER nurse called me to say they were still working on Greg in the emergency room, and he would be admitted. Someone would call to give me more information, but that was all she knew at the moment. She added that from that point forward, Greg could no longer use his phone to text or call, but they would send his phone with him to his room. Before she ended the conversation she asked if we had our advance directive registered with the hospital system. Her question caused a surge of angst to rise within me. As wise as it is to have an advance directive, we hadn't imagined needing it now. They must be anticipating the end of Greg's life. By the time the call ended, my anxiety had reached new levels, especially since I didn't know all the details of his condition.

There were more family texts and calls. Considering the medical decisions that would need to be made and the seriousness of my husband's condition, Greg Jr. thought it best if he could connect with the medical staff in the ER and requested that I give them his cell phone number the next time they called me. I was glad he would be leading the way in discussions with the medical team. He would know the right questions to ask, and we would receive more definitive information.

Thankfully, shortly after 3:30 p.m., the nurse called again. This time, she gave me a little more detail. Among other things, Greg's biggest problem was pneumonia in both lungs. Also, a blood test showed he had an infection, probably due to his lungs. They planned to admit him and place him in isolation. Some tests had not yet come back, so they awaited further analysis. That was all the information we were able to obtain.

Pneumonia in both lungs? Other infections? Those were symptoms only mentioned in the worst cases of COVID reported by the CDC. Is that what he was suffering from? The questions and concerns for his condition overwhelmed my thoughts.

At approximately 5:00 p.m., my son put together a family conference call. The nurse had contacted him with more details and clarification about his dad's condition. Their diagnosis for Greg was respiratory failure with double pneumonia. He had to be sedated and intubated in an effort to save his life. They would move him to the new COVID ICU to be placed on a ventilator. The decision was made to treat him as though he had the coronavirus, although the test results had not yet come back. Unknown to us at that point, Greg was the first COVID-19 patient at that hospital to go on a ventilator.

Unknown to us at that point, Greg was the first COVID-19 patient at that hospital to go on a ventilator.

Heaviness pressed on my heart like massive rocks avalanching onto my chest. All I could think to say was, "Okay, we've got to pray intensely for Daddy."

Hollie said she would begin a prayer vigil with me from where she lived—we could call each other at any time, and she would walk through this night with me.

We continued waiting for the doctor to call. The nurses had contacted us. They repeated that sometime soon I would hear from the doctor. The minutes dragged on at the speed of rush hour traffic in New York City, and finally another hour had passed. As we waited in anxious anticipation, our prayers for Greg intensified.

In the meantime, Greg Jr. and Lesley decided it would be wisest for him to fly to Springfield, Missouri, as soon as possible to be close to us and assist however he could. He would get a hotel room close to the hospital where his dad lay in ICU. Greg Jr. was able to leave San Diego at 8:50 that evening (Central Time).

Almost as soon as Greg Jr. boarded the plane, my phone rang. It was the hospital.

The doctor's voice sounded weary. "I just want to give you a rundown on where we are with your husband. He's been admitted, as you know. He's in COVID ICU. He's been intubated. We had some complications inserting the first tube, so we ended up using a smaller one. In the process, your husband lost some oxygen." Then he repeated the facts we knew about double pneumonia and respiratory failure. He made clear that the whole situation didn't look good at all, then added, "You will probably get a call sometime before morning."

When I asked him to explain what he meant, he answered, "Like I said, we've done all we can for him. There's nothing more we know of to help him. He's very, very sick. His lungs have been compromised, and he may not make it. I'm so sorry, ma'am."

I couldn't breathe. Although almost suffocating, I managed to choke out, "You're saying there's no hope for him?"

His calm professional voice repeated succinctly, "All I'm saying is we've done all we can. The situation is very, very serious, and because of his lungs, we do *not* know if he can pull through."

A million questions filled my mind, but I was dumbstruck. It was as though someone had stuffed a wad of stockings down my throat. Somehow, I managed to grunt out, "Oh, no. It's that bad?. . . Thank you, sir, for calling."

I remember falling onto the couch again and sobbing, "I can't

> **"We've done all we can for him. There's nothing more we know of to help him. He's very, very sick."**

lose him. No!" Tears streamed down my face as I held on to my stomach. I was nauseous and couldn't swallow. The pain of the doctor's words pierced every part of my body, especially my chest, which felt like more rocks were pounding on top of it.

I called Hollie, Lesley, and my sisters. I also called Kevin and our pastor. It comforted me to know my family and friends were interceding with me. Through those hours, we clung to each other for support and hope. Hollie was faithful to her promise to stay up with me the entire night, making herself available for prayer or conversation, whatever I needed. The doctor's call had left us troubled and burdened. She prevailed beside me through this, although thousands of miles separated us.

Not only did Hollie stay awake, but her daughter Audrey, who was fourteen at the time, insisted she would stay up with her mom too and pray. Hollie described it this way: "Audrey came down to the living room when I was awake that entire night and when we thought my dad was going to die. She knelt on the floor by our couch and prayed for hours on end as I talked to my mom. I kept trying to tell her, 'Go to bed,' but she said, 'No, no, I need to pray. I need to pray.' I'll never forget that picture—seeing her pray for her grandfather and her grandmother and the entire situation. Her intercessory prayer was very moving."

I hurt for my grandchildren, who love their grandfather so much. Without a doubt, they had sensed his fervent love for them all their lives. They had enjoyed countless moments of laughter, and I'm sure they will always know him as the grandparent who led the way in games and sports with them.

Our vacation in Bali in 2018 was a perfect example. We had rented an Airbnb big enough for all fourteen of us. It was a blast. The property included a beautiful pool just for our family that overlooked the Pacific Ocean. Every day, we spent hours in that pool. Talk about hilarious—nothing was funnier than when Papa joined in the "raft competition," where you had to jump from the edge of the pool onto each of four rafts in a series of jumps without falling into the water. Now imagine a six-foot-four, 235-pound, 68-year-old man trying to jump that far into the water, leap from one raft to the next without falling off, until he reached the last one! He was determined to play right along with his grandchildren—his buddies. I smiled as I remembered the laughter that day. Our family still talks about it.

The time Greg invested in his grandchildren's lives was paying off in a big way now. All of his eight grandchildren were interceding in prayer for him.

About 11:00 that night, Lesley called me. "Would it be okay if we had a little prayer meeting? We can set up a call to include anybody available at Hollie's." Lesley's sister and brother-in-law are pastors in their hometown of San Diego, and they had come to Lesley's house to bring comfort to her and our grandchildren.

At that time, it would have been 7:00 in the morning where Hollie was. Since Jason had returned to Israel from abroad, his required quarantine took place in an apartment below his family's. He had also stayed awake to pray for Greg, so he was able to join the conference call. Audrey was part of the call as well as our four grandchildren in California.

In unity, we sang hymns and songs of worship and sensed the Lord's nearness. God's amazing presence surrounded us. My voice was so raw from crying and talking to so many people throughout the day and night that I could barely sing. But as I listened to the beautiful voices—most of them my grandchildren's—singing worship songs as loudly as they could and praying for their papa, it moved me in ways I cannot describe.

I laid down on the couch and closed my eyes while the voices of my family washed over me like a healing balm. Each grandchild prayed that their papa would not die. It seemed like a heavenly sound coming through the phone as their voices joined in heartfelt worship, lifted the name of Jesus, and cried out for His power to heal.

A few minutes after our prayer meeting ended, my phone rang. Greg Jr. let me know he had landed in St. Louis and was going to get a ride to Springfield. He sounded cheerful. He had contacted the hospital and learned his dad was still alive. His condition hadn't changed, but he was alive. He'd made it this far.

We spread the news to our family through text messaging. Greg Jr.'s call had brought some relief to my mind. Yet the doctor had said they could call *anytime* during the night, and the night was far from over.

"This is hard, but this is a good sign," Greg Jr. encouraged us. "Dad made it from this afternoon until tonight. Let's keep praying. Let's believe you will not get a call in the middle of the night and Dad will make it through."

As I lay on the couch after we disconnected, my mind was full of the memory of our worship time during our phone prayer meeting. Thoughts of my grandchildren praying and singing with their beautiful voices brought hope to my heart. I meditated on that, and somehow, I fell asleep.

The phone rang again. It was 6:30 a.m. I hadn't received a call saying Greg had passed away, but was this *that call*? Since the phone had stayed near me all night, I glanced at the screen. It wasn't the hospital, but Greg Jr. Had they called him first with the bad news?

I listened carefully to his voice trying to discern his frame of mind. He didn't sound sad or worried. He let me know he had made it to Springfield and checked into the hotel since he wasn't allowed to stay with me. The first thing he did when he arrived in Springfield was contact the ICU. He could hardly contain himself as he said, "Dad made it through the entire night. He's hanging in there!"

Together on the phone with the family, we had a time of jubilation, with more tears—but this time tears of joy. My son put it this way: "Mom, do you understand what this means from a medical perspective? Dad had been given only a ten percent chance by the medical staff and doctors to make it through the night. He beat those odds and lived through the horrendous first 24 hours of his condition. This is a huge milestone for him. We certainly have reason to rejoice." And that's exactly what we did.

> **"This is a huge milestone for him. We certainly have reason to rejoice."**

After we hung up, I walked to the window. The sun peeked over the horizon, and hope arose with the dawning of a new day. Greg had beat the odds. The grim report had caused agonizing hours throughout the night, but the prayers and songs of praise sustained us and helped us to endure. My heart warmed as I remembered how my grandchildren had called out to God, and Audrey insisted she had to stay up and pray for her papa. There was no doubt in my mind that what is impossible with man is possible with God. The words of Psalm 30:5 resonated in my heart: *"Weeping may stay for the night, but rejoicing comes in the morning."*

As I turned away from the window, I sincerely hoped that today would bring more good news. But I had no idea of the battle that would soon follow.

"DO NOT BE AFRAID!
DON'T BE DISCOURAGED BY
THIS MIGHTY ARMY,

FOR THE BATTLE IS NOT
YOURS, BUT GOD'S."

2 CHRONICLES 20:15 NLT

CHAPTER THREE

Battle Rages

ON THIS SUNNY BUT cold March Tuesday, I praised God for the miracle that Greg had survived his first very critical night of hospitalization. I basked in the joy that he was still alive. It was such a relief to know Greg Jr. could now be in the hospital, somewhere near his dad's ICU room, although we understood he couldn't enter the quarantined room due to active COVID.

As the morning progressed, the reality of Greg's dire condition haunted me. Was there such a thing as "cautious hope," or was it the same as lack of faith? Questions filled my mind all morning. Why was my hope not extravagant after Greg survived his first night with only a ten-percent chance to live? I gave the Lord all the credit for that miracle, and yet doubts pricked my mind. He could still die today or tomorrow or next week, because his critical condition hadn't changed.

Was I dishonoring the Lord because of my cautious hope? The famous words of Thomas Aquinas came to my mind: "Faith has to do with things that are not seen and hope with things that are not at hand."[1] That made sense to me, and I pondered those words.

---

1   Thomas Aquinas Quotes. BrainyQuote.com, BrainyMedia Inc., 2022. Accessed December 17, 2022. https://www.brainyquote.com/quotes/

In so doing, I remembered Psalm 62:5, which reminded me *Who* my source of hope is. "For God alone, O my soul, wait in silence, for my hope is from him. He only is my rock and my salvation, my fortress; I shall not be shaken" (ESV).

This certainly was clear and direct. The answer for increased hope lies in the One who brought that miracle yesterday. In silent prayer, I committed to seek Him more every day for the hope I lacked, and to trust Him through this journey no matter the outcome.

I had read that verse often for many years, and now it illuminated my mind—and oddly enough, comforted me—so that now, even though I felt a cautious hope, I didn't have to stay there. Each time I struggled with doubt, especially when the news or prognosis wasn't good, I could regain hope as I refocused my gaze on God.

My thoughts were interrupted by the phone ringing. It was Greg Jr. letting me know he was at the hospital. He explained that the hospital allowed him to stay on the COVID ICU floor. They set up a small desk outside of Greg's room which had large windows into the hallway covered with huge warning stickers and tape. Some warnings were: "No Entrance," "Isolation," and "Keep Out." He was told his dad was in the same condition as the night before. The doctors had no idea how Greg had made it through his first night, but they were encouraged that he was still alive. My son sent me a picture and a video of his dad, which he took through the window of Greg's room.

---

thomas_aquinas_192518

Greg lay on his back, his head gently tilted to the right, with a breathing tube and a feeding tube in place. He was covered with blankets and didn't seem to be in any pain. As I stared at the picture, it made me sick to my stomach. He looked like he was hooked up to something on every part of his body—machines on both sides, and even behind him. It crushed me to see him lying there, appearing lifeless and oblivious to his surroundings. How could this strong man who had been busy just a week ago, conducting interviews for new global workers and chairing a board meeting, be so helpless a few days later?

Greg Jr. told me he would arrive at my house that afternoon. Our plan was to meet in the garage, two cars apart. Our church lent us a space heater so we could endure the chilly air.

Thinking about his visit, odd as it would have to be, still brought great joy. I knew exactly what I would do. I pulled out flour, sugar, eggs, and the rest of the ingredients to make chocolate chip cookies for him to take back to his hotel room. As I reached for the first ingredient to put in the bowl, my phone rang. It was the nurse from our insurance company.

She asked a lot of questions but was very kind. She said she'd be calling me often and would take care of us. The insurance would cover our expenses. There was no need to worry, she told me. Greg was placed in the champion program, which meant he would receive first-rate attention and care throughout his entire recovery.

Talking to her was almost like talking to a friend—she was *that* personable. So, in our conversation, I mentioned that our son was in town and staying in a hotel near the hospital.

I explained that he is a physician and, therefore, was permitted into the medical facilities. I proceeded to tell her about the chocolate chip cookies I was about to bake for him.

She politely canceled that plan. "Oh, I'm so sorry, but you can't make cookies for your son." Then she explained that nothing made in my house could be given to others.

My shoulders slumped. I had imagined Greg Jr.'s joy when I handed him the cookies, and it had brightened my morning. My expression of love was snatched way. I should have realized, of course, that it would not be permitted, but with all the changing rules, it was difficult to remember them all.

Instead of baking, I started to clean everything—the entire house. I pulled on gloves and cleaned every room except the master bedroom. Every time I looked in there, I thought of Greg's last night before he was taken to the emergency room. I couldn't bring myself to go in, at least not today. Although I couldn't be sure Greg had COVID, I was fairly certain he did. I'd researched the potential devastation of this virus. It was insidious in rocking the world off kilter. I feared what lurked in our master bedroom. The bedsheets needed to be removed and washed, and the entire room had to be cleaned. However, it felt like I would be confronting an enemy on a battlefield while uncertain which weapons would be effective. That room could wait.

While I cleaned the rest of the house, I turned on the news. A reporter announced that busy American cities were becoming deserted as the nation implemented new, dramatic restrictions to contain COVID-19. The more details I heard, the more perplexed I became. The situation was worsening every single day.

I had almost reached the end of my cleaning project when the doorbell rang. I couldn't answer it, of course, so I strolled to the window to look out. A dear friend stood and waved at me.

I smiled and waved back, all the while wishing I could throw the door open, invite her in, and sit for a chat.

She showed me the box of food in her hand, and then motioned that she would leave it on the porch. She waved again when she reached her car and put her hands together to let me know she was praying, and then she drove off.

When groceries were delivered by a store, there was an exact protocol to sanitize every item while wearing plastic gloves.

Delivery procedures were one of the new restrictions. People who ordered groceries could look up the protocol on the CDC's website to learn how to receive food left on their doorsteps. When groceries were delivered by a store, there was an exact protocol to sanitize every item while wearing plastic gloves. Even the bags the groceries arrived in had to be properly disposed of. Everyone would be busy with these new cleaning methods in an attempt to fight this ferocious virus.

Laying all these concerns aside, I cheered myself with the thought of my son's soon arrival.

When I heard the garage door begin to open, I hurried to see him. Even if the circumstances were peculiar, it was great to be in the same room and talk with him. It seemed cruel and unnatural that we couldn't hug each other.

Greg Jr. reviewed his dad's condition of that day with me. His kidneys weren't functioning well; he retained fluids, so his doctor talked about the possible need for dialysis. His lungs were still in critical condition and very compromised.

My thoughts swirled. Were Greg's kidneys in jeopardy now? How could this possibly be happening? Dialysis? Then my mind returned to the questions about hope and faith. Did fear of the "worst news" give me permission to entertain a cautious hope? But what more would my husband have to endure? I felt overwhelmed, like I would suffocate. Kidney failure, dialysis—it left me breathless.

> **Did fear of the "worst news" give me permission to entertain a cautious hope?**

Greg Jr. must have noticed the agony on my face, because he tried to cheer me up. He texted a picture to me of lungs drawn by my granddaughter, Emery, his oldest child. She was fifteen years old. She had created an accurate drawing of healthy lungs, and she prayed over the picture every day, many times a day, asking that her papa's lungs would be healed. She hung it in her bedroom where she did her school by Zoom. Her prayers for Papa's sick lungs were a part of her everyday routine.

Emery's love and dedication to pray for her papa moved me deeply, and especially now that he had taken a turn for the worse. I only wished we could tell Greg how much love was being poured out on him by every family member.

As I lay my weary head on my pillow that night, I asked the Giver of Hope for more hope and faith. Greg Jr. had called to let me know that dialysis had indeed begun. I could hear the disappointment in his voice and my heart sank in despair. He also let me know that he started posting his dad's journey on Facebook. He wanted me to look at the post when I felt up to it. I snuggled deeper under my warm blanket in our guest room, clicked on my Facebook account, and began reading.

> The perspective that God has given me, however, is of a man who knows what it means to have peace, who is comfortable in uncertainty, whose faith does not waver with circumstances, and who is battling for one more day on earth to share God's grace one more time. I don't see my father as a broken man in a hospital room but one equipped and battling.

Looking again at Emery's picture of the lungs, tears ran down my face, and I prayed.

Perhaps it was because of the last words I read the night before about "equipped and battling," but when I awoke on Wednesday morning, I felt like I had physically and mentally battled enemy giants. The fact that Greg was on dialysis didn't help matters and pierced my soul like a dagger. It could have been that my emotions were aggravated by the fact that I had slept in the guest room and missed my bed.

After a quick breakfast and time reading my Bible, Hollie and I talked for a while. She continued to be available to me any time, day or night, for which I was very grateful. Her calls were so important to me. I sensed the strength of her faith and how much she cared for both her dad and me. Her wisdom and prayers lifted me.

I told her how anxious I was as I anticipated a report on Greg's night. Greg Jr. would call when he could, but since I was unable to see Greg, touch him, or stand beside him as I prayed for him, it ate at me like locusts on a field of wheat.

I confided in Hollie that as much as I wanted to clean our bedroom, I couldn't bring myself to do it. I explained the reasons why I simply couldn't. Not yet. Maybe I would try again today.

When Greg Jr. called, he let me know they had already been able to drain two liters of liquid from Greg's body, his kidneys had improved a bit, and his labs were slightly better. They started him on hydroxychloroquine.

I was so grateful Greg's kidneys had already improved somewhat. Perhaps we would see a consistent positive pattern each day now. My hope was on the rise.

The rest of the day, I answered texts, phone calls, and emails. My sisters and sisters-in-law, all of whom lived in other cities, were tenacious about staying in touch and sending Bible verses. They enlisted prayer from their friends, churches, and acquaintances all over the country.

Greg Jr.'s first social media post had already reached a worldwide audience. Now friends and strangers alike checked in to read about possibly one of the first victims of COVID on a vent in the United States. We weren't yet certain if Greg had COVID, but everything seemed to point in that direction. Due to social media, the number of people who were concerned increased, and the needed prayers steadily multiplied.

Since we had lived in Austria for eighteen years, led AG Missions in Europe for another thirteen years, and then traveled around the world the past nine years when Greg assumed the responsibility of Executive Director, we developed relationships with churches, pastors, and other workers globally. Naturally, we acquired a great many friends and acquaintances whom we loved and gladly served. Now, they blessed us with their earnest prayers and intercessions on my husband's behalf.

This humbled me and moved me to tears. An army of prayer warriors had joined our family in this fight for Greg's life.

Later that day, Greg Jr. brought me an early dinner wrapped in a box. All day, he had peered at his dad through a window as he quietly prayed and sang worship songs. He also participated in some important discussions with the medical team about his dad's uncertain and critical condition.

My son and I sat on folding chairs in our scroungy garage-turned-living-room, two car widths apart, with a space heater that offered some warmth. We adapted to our new circumstances for the opportunity to spend some time together and talk.

We didn't often have time for many soul-to-soul discussions once our children became adults, lived in other cities, and were busy with growing families and careers of their own. However, in the midst of our major concerns and deepest heartache, this predicament had given us such a gift. Those "garage dates" with

Greg Jr. and the "phone dates" with Hollie became precious and comforted us.

A few hours after Greg Jr. left and returned to his hotel, he called to let me know his dad had indeed tested positive for COVID.

That night, while on the phone with Hollie, we wondered what the future would look like as Greg's body fought to expel the virus. While we talked, I became aware of discomfort in my body. I felt sick and achy. My head began to hurt, I noticed a slight earache, and felt jittery. Hollie suggested I take my temperature to see if I had a fever.

The thermometer showed I had a low-grade fever of 99 degrees. We agreed this sounded a lot like the symptoms my husband had developed almost a week ago.

Hollie and Greg Jr. encouraged me to go to the hospital to treat it quickly before it spiraled. I feared their assessment was accurate, so I agreed. But how would I get there? I couldn't call a taxi or Uber since neither were available in Springfield during the pandemic. Greg Jr. wasn't allowed to pick me up, nor could friends take me in their cars without violating the six-foot social distancing protocol. I only had one option—I had to drive myself. Although I felt sick, I had my wits about me, so I convinced Hollie and Greg Jr. that I could drive to the hospital. They conceded with the promise that one of them would always stay on the phone with me.

At 9:30 p.m., I headed to the local hospital where Greg lay in the ICU. Despite the fact that it was 5:30 a.m. where Hollie lived, she was on the phone with me until I arrived.

Triage protocol was changing from day to day, so the emergency room was crowded with a line of people like me who suspected they had COVID, as well as another line for those who had other needs. The two lines were more than six feet apart, and masks were required. Both lines had stickers on the floor to keep incoming patients six feet apart. Everyone's temperature was taken.

After they checked to see if I had a fever, they escorted me to a room and left. There were no other occupants in the room. It was obvious that I was in an unused part of the hospital. I felt certain the room I was in was not a normal patient's room. Instead of a door, a large curtain was pulled to shut me in. I heard voices in a nearby hallway. It reminded me of an old '70s Communist-country waiting room I had been in during our years in Europe—barren, old flooring worn with age, no closet. It was more like a storage room they had emptied out and were now using for patients. I chuckled and thanked God that I at least had some experience with this type of setting, so it didn't scare me as it might others.

It's interesting how fleeting memories, almost forgotten, can strengthen and encourage. As I glanced around the room, I remembered our time in Budapest, Hungary, where we had attended a Eurasian global workers' meeting many years earlier. Greg and I, as well as our friend, Paul, an AGWM worker living in Hungary, stopped at an airport to pick up Doug, another worker from the Middle East. Doug was in the process of putting his suitcase in the trunk of our car when a strong gust of wind knocked the trunk door on his head. It left a huge gash above his right eye. A profuse amount of blood gushed out. We grabbed a couple of clean rags we kept in the car and put them on the gaping wound. We told him to keep firm pressure on it and then took off to seek help.

I was so glad Paul was with us. Since he lived in Hungary, he knew how to direct us to the closest hospital. We drove as fast as we could while Doug continued to hold towels to his injury. When we arrived at the hospital, we discovered it was only partially open. The attendant in charge was so intoxicated that he made no sense. His hands trembled. How was he supposed to hold an examination tool? We couldn't allow this man to attempt stitching Doug's wound.

Instead, we returned to the car and headed to the next closest hospital. It was rather small. The doctor in charge informed us that he was not equipped to stitch a wound, and no one else was available.

As we re-entered the car, we feared for Doug. His increased weakness let us know he had lost a lot of blood. Paul said we'd better head to the main hospital although it was several miles down the road. The pressure to get help for Doug as fast as possible sped us along. If only the traffic would cooperate. Finally, we arrived at the main hospital, which was really a campus. Each medical discipline had a separate building. And we had a problem. There were no signs on the buildings to identify them. Where was the emergency room? We couldn't waste any more time, so we parked and entered the first building with an unlocked door.

Paul and Greg each held onto one of Doug's arms and helped walk him through the doors and to the elevator. We got off at the first floor. As we exited, we faced a long, dark, windowless hallway. It wasn't empty. There were many women in sleeping attire who walked with slow steps along the hall or sat on old, dilapidated wooden benches. We ignored the scene and searched for anyone who looked like a nurse or a doctor.

Paul spotted a doctor coming out of a room. Thankfully, Paul spoke Hungarian and explained our situation, asking the doctor to please help our friend.

The doctor half laughed as he informed us that we were on the maternity floor, and they weren't set up for these types of emergencies. However, when Paul showed him Doug's gash, he readily agreed to take care of him.

A few minutes later, we were taken to a room that reminded me of the room I now occupied—except that the room in Budapest was worse. Metal wardrobes with dents and chips lined one wall. There were cracks and drains on the cement floor. An old, raggedy upholstered chair sat in a corner. The room in Budapest was scary.

They helped Doug onto the only bed in the room. It had stirrups at one end for women in labor as they prepared to deliver their babies.

I smiled as I recalled this memory. There lay Doug with his large feet in archaic leather stirrups. The gynecologist who stitched him up did a great job. He said, "Well, all these years of stitching up women has paid off today. I doubt you will even have a scar."

Then, the four of us marched out of the delivery room and back down the long hallway as curious women stared. The shocked and wide-eyed glances at Doug's huge bandage over his eye followed us to the elevator.

I shook my head at the memory, amazed at how well it all turned out. The last time we saw Doug, the scar was barely noticeable.

Now, here we were in another crisis. But how would it all end? I checked my watch. It felt like an eternity passed as I waited for a doctor or nurse to finally arrive. Where was the ICU unit and how close was I to Greg? Was there any way I could escape this dismal room and find the floor he was on?

At last, a doctor and a nurse pulled back the curtains and entered my room wearing hazmat suits. I couldn't see their faces. A chill raced through my body that had nothing to do with a fever.

I had to undergo the uncomfortable COVID test with a long ear-swab-like stick pushed deep into my nostrils. After they checked my temperature, they informed me it wasn't very high. However, Greg Jr. (who wasn't allowed to come into my room) had called them and insisted that I be treated with hydroxy-chloroquine and two antibiotics. These were especially important since I have asthma and diabetes. Then they sent me home with instructions to watch for shortness of breath, respiratory issues, a cough (which I always have due to asthma), and low oxygen levels (90 or lower). If any of those symptoms occurred, I should contact my primary care doctor immediately.

As I climbed back into my car, I called Hollie as promised, and we talked the whole way home. It was 12:30 a.m. on Thursday as I pulled into my garage. I was exhausted.

If I thought I had awakened yesterday feeling like I'd fought in a roaring battle, Thursday morning was an all-out war! I woke throughout the night moaning in pain and shivering. It felt as though someone had pushed me into a freezer. I had severe body aches that reminded me of labor pains except that they were throughout my body. Two blankets weren't enough to stop the chills. My throat hurt. I mustered enough strength to take my temperature and saw it had climbed to 101 degrees. Next, I checked my oxygen level. It was 88. I had to alert my primary care doctor. I also called Greg Jr. and Hollie, who insisted I go to the hospital. Greg Jr. called an ambulance and informed the hospital that I was on my way back.

Low oxygen levels were the main concern. I felt weak and very tired. I found myself once again in the "scary room" from the night before, but without the endless wait. Not long after admittance, I was taken to my room on the newly-converted COVID floor for patients who were not in critical condition. The annoying squeak of the hazmat suits that hospital personnel wore as they wheeled me to my room added to my already-severe headache. I vaguely remember squealing in pain as they shifted me from one bed to another, but I must have fallen asleep soon after, because the next thing I remember was waking up in a new room.

No one had been in to check on me in quite a while. The doctor in admittance had said it would take at least two days to receive the results of my COVID test. Even though by all appearances I had contracted the virus from my husband, verification would bring closure to the uncertainty.

It's hard to believe that one week brought this much change.

So, when Greg Jr. called to let me know he was going to get some food, I shuffled to the window to wave.

When he returned from his lunch, he called to inform me that Greg's sedation and vent settings had been lowered. The nurse said he wiggled his toes. There was even a chance his endotracheal tube would come out. We'd been waiting desperately for good news, and now it felt as though a heavy weight had been lifted off our shoulders.

Despite the aching pain in my face, I smiled and gave praise to God. One week ago that day, Greg became ill, and then four days later, he ended up in the ICU with COVID, fighting for his life. We weren't out of the woods yet, so I continued to cling to the Lord, my only hope in this awful battle.

As I lay there, I remembered a haunting incident back in April of 2019, almost a year ago. Greg and I were in Kenya, Africa, for special meetings with our Missiology Committee, whose purpose was to address present missiological issues in AGWM. This was an annual gathering and one my husband highly valued and spent much time in prayer about before attending.

We had stayed in this hotel many times and enjoyed its old English roots and history. In fact, we'd previously stayed in the exact room assigned to us on this trip. But as soon as we walked into that room, something felt different . . . weird . . . disturbing. We both sensed it and tried to ignore it, but we couldn't. From the first night there to the moment we got back on the airplane four days later, we were plagued with a sense of evil all around us. We couldn't see it, but it was everywhere, like a dark shadow that followed our every step.

A few weeks before, several of our colleagues as well as Greg and I were inundated with filthy and lewd email pop-ups. They were out of control and all day long. We were deleting them constantly. That's exactly how the evil in that room felt. It was like a demon was following us, trying to kill us. We tried to eradicate it.

Not only was the feeling in the room a strange experience like nothing we'd ever encountered before, but it was frightening. A living horror. It felt as though the devil had clutched us in his grasp, hissing and laughing at us. No matter where we went, even in our meetings, we felt the hellish mocking. We looked at each other in despair as we wondered when and how this would end.

This spiritual battle continued day and night throughout that trip. It exhausted us and depleted our energy.

From our first night in Kenya until the day we left, because of the strength of the evil presence around us, we sang hymns and worship songs. When we went to bed, we asked God to forgive us for any wrong we might have done and asked Him to tell us if we were going in the wrong direction in ministry. We read Scripture aloud and laid open Bibles on our chests. We both cried out to the Lord. We rebuked the devil in the name of Jesus, our Lord.

Psalm 91 became our anchor. We read it morning, noon, and night. We also read it several times as we tried to fall asleep each night.

When we finally left Africa, we were exhausted, confused, and our spirits felt broken. But we had gained a deeper understanding of what it meant to place our complete trust in God—total dependence on Him.

Greg and I bonded more than ever and grew even closer to each other after that trip because of our many discussions as we continued to process the horrors of the spiritual warfare we'd encountered. We pledged to read Psalm 91 and other Scriptures every day.

And now, this day in the hospital was no different. Despite the frailty and pain I felt as I lay in the hospital bed, I read Psalm 91 again and remembered our African trip as if it had been yesterday.

1 Whoever dwells in the shelter of the Most High
will rest in the shadow of the Almighty.
2 I will say of the LORD, "He is my refuge and my fortress,
my God, in whom I trust."

3 Surely he will save you
from the fowler's snare
and from the deadly pestilence.
4 He will cover you with his feathers,
and under his wings you will find refuge;
his faithfulness will be your shield and rampart.
5 You will not fear the terror of night,

nor the arrow that flies by day,
6 nor the pestilence that stalks in the darkness,
nor the plague that destroys at midday.
7 A thousand may fall at your side,
ten thousand at your right hand,
but it will not come near you.
8 You will only observe with your eyes
and see the punishment of the wicked.

9 If you say, "The Lord is my refuge,"
and you make the Most High your dwelling,
10 no harm will overtake you,
no disaster will come near your tent.
11 For he will command his angels concerning you
to guard you in all your ways;
12 they will lift you up in their hands,
so that you will not strike your foot against a stone.
13 You will tread on the lion and the cobra;
you will trample the great lion and the serpent.

14 "Because he loves me," says the Lord, "I will rescue him;
I will protect him, for he acknowledges my name.
15 He will call on me, and I will answer him;
I will be with him in trouble,
I will deliver him and honor him.
16 With long life I will satisfy him
and show him my salvation."

Could it be that God had begun to prepare us during the previous year to battle this deadly virus that would attack our family, as well as the lives of so many others? I believe that's exactly what He did.

Verses 5–7 of that chapter spoke exactly to our one-on-one with Satan through those horror-filled days in Kenya. And as I read them now, I felt overwhelmed with thankfulness to the Lord, for I realized He had provided us with a spiritual heads-up even while we were yet in Kenya for this battle we now faced. Tears flowed down my face as peace welled up in my soul.

I love the entire psalm. The verses cannot be separated, because one leads powerfully to the next. However, at this moment, as I reminisced about the past and endured the present, I clearly understood verses 1 to 13, for I had lived them. God was our refuge those days and nights in Africa. He covered and protected us with His wings. But now I clung to verses 14 through 16 as I faced our present battle.

The Lord knew all about COVID before it hit. He knew I would have to face this moment without my husband to pray beside me. But since God knew, He prepared me.

I told the Lord how much I loved Him. I called out to my Deliverer who had spared our lives and our sanity in Kenya while we clung to Him. As I now prayed in my lonely, barren, sterile hospital room, the Holy Spirit entered and renewed my spirit. I pledged again that I would never stop trusting Him. I would not cease to call on Him and His powerful name.

On Friday morning, I awoke to a poke in my arm, followed by more pokes. I didn't bother to attempt a conversation with the nurses because it was much too difficult to hear them through their hazmat masks.

Unable to fall back asleep, I checked my phone for any new text messages. My daughter had posted in our family text. It was a text directed to her dad.

To my one and only Daddy. One of my favorite things about you is that ever since I can remember, you have started your day with abiding. I have clear pictures in my mind of all the homes we lived in growing up. Waking up to you reading the Word, praying, worshiping the Lord in song. I used to wonder at you being able to get up so early every single day and devote yourself to this precious time with your Savior. And now my kids do the same. They love to talk about waking up to their Papa with his Bose headphones on, singing praises out loud to Jesus. They ask me before each of your visits, "Do you think Papa will sing these songs when he visits this time?" And as you are lying in your hospital bed, fully sedated, breathing through a machine, I picture you praising Jesus in song. It's simply who you are. It's your spiritual blood flow. You and I love Christmas songs, and when we are together over Christmas, we talk about the latest Christmas albums and songs that mean something to us. So, this is my song for you, my prayer for you, Daddy, simple and pure—our favorite kind. He is your breath of heaven. I love you. Hollie.

And then she posted a link to the song, "Breath of Heaven," sung by Amy Grant and written by Chris Eaton.

As I read Hollie's text, I could see in my mind's eye the many times Greg sat in his chair, headphones on, and sang songs of praise to God. Even when we traveled, that was his routine. It filled my heart with joy and moved me to tears that my children and grandchildren had such precious memories of Greg. It was a gift he had unknowingly given them.

Hollie had accurately described her dad's daily *abiding* routine. It felt like such a long time since I had seen Greg. I missed the sound of his voice as he sang one of his favorite songs. I missed waking up to see his tear-filled eyes as he prayed for the many people on his prayer list. I had taken his daily habits for granted, but now I would do anything to have one more day to pray and sing and discuss Bible passages together with him.

As he lay intubated on his hospital ICU bed, did he sing in his thoughts the songs he loved so much? Was he able to meditate on Psalm 91? Did he realize how prophetic that psalm now appeared?

I opened my playlist and soon the song "Breath of Heaven" filled my room. Although I had listened to it countless times, it still moved me, and especially now. These words have great meaning. Jesus brings light to every dismal place and I needed and wanted His holiness to fill my mind, my soul, and my thoughts. I prayed those anointed words over Greg and myself, and then worshiped God.

The door to my room opened and a nurse stepped in to inform me that my COVID test results had come back positive.

Well, no shock, of course. As sick as I felt, there had been no doubt in my mind that I also had COVID.

Reports of the ever-increasing spread of the coronavirus filled the news. Everyone reported that this virus had forced millions of Americans into virtual lockdown.

Over 75 million people in New York City, California, Illinois, and Connecticut were ordered to stay home.[2]

US borders to Canada and Mexico were set to close to nonessential travel.[3]

People everywhere were scared. The government was floundering, trying to figure out how to deal with such a deadly virus.

2   "75 Million Americans Told to Stay Home as Testing Reveals More Coronavirus Cases," CNN, March 21, 2020. https://wsvn.com/news/politics/75-million-americans-told-to-stay-home-as-testing-reveals-more-coronavirus-cases/.

3   Alvarez, Priscilla, et. al. "Trump Administration Limits Nonessential Travel between US and Mexico." CNN, March 20, 2020. https://www.cnn.com/2020/03/20/politics/us-mexico-border/index.html.

A little while later, Greg Jr. called to inform me that the CDC had announced that California was a hot spot for COVID. Since that was his home state, he would have to leave the hospital and quarantine for two weeks. If he had no symptoms after that time, he could return to the hospital. As we discussed the new regulations and his quarantine, it seemed to me that he should go home. After all, he couldn't be with me or in the hospital with Greg, so why spend the money on a hotel? He might as well go back to his family in California and be secure there as COVID ravaged every state.

Saturday arrived with the realization that we faced an up and downhill battle. The ICU staff had tried to lower Greg's ventilator settings when it seemed he'd be able to tolerate it. Unfortunately, as the sedation was decreased, Greg's lungs didn't respond well. They soon realized he required more support from the vent, so the settings had to be increased again. In addition, he was still on dialysis, but at least his kidneys were responding.

Prayer support increased as Greg Jr. posted daily about his dad's condition, and the number of comments and reactions on Facebook posts soared. In fact, the Facebook posts came to the attention of national TV and radio stations, and they requested interviews. Greg Jr. received invitations from sources like NBC, ABC, Inside Edition, Dr. Oz, and local stations around the United States. From his hotel room, he discussed the particulars of his parent's encounter with COVID, not only from a medical perspective, but also that of a son.

Greg Jr. had spent a lot of time with the staff in the ICU and saw their dedication twenty-four hours a day. He made this observation in his Facebook post:

> The nursing staff has been unbelievable and opened my eyes to the potential crisis that we face. It takes 2 nurses to care for my dad. One inside his room, geared up with anti-viral suits (these guys all watched Apollo 13), doing all the work with the IVs keeping him hydrated, the tube feeds keeping him nourished, moving him left to right and tucking pillows to avoid bed ulcers, managing his endotracheal tube to make sure his airway is secured, tracking his urine output, giving baths, and administering his life-saving medications. The other must stand watch outside the room to ensure the one in the room is okay, and when there is need for other supplies there has to be a "sterile" exchange. WE MUST protect our nursing staff and our respiratory therapists. If you are a nurse or RT, we have to protect you!!! Stay healthy, please do everything you must to avoid infection or requiring to be quarantined.

Our family's battle against COVID raged on, with somewhat good days followed by grim days. Battle lines changed on a continual basis. We seemed to win some battles, but they were soon followed by defeats, which made us aware of our need for reinforcements.

On Sunday, my fever spiked, so they extended my hospital stay. I had intermittent respiratory issues, and with the continued pain, they started me on two more antibiotics to prevent secondary infections.

The ICU medical team allowed our family, one by one, to talk to Greg on the speakerphone. It was an awkward and strange experience. I talked for about ten minutes like I was giving a speech to an unresponsive audience. I pushed past the discomfort and began to tell Greg how much I loved him, how I missed him, and that he was never out of my thoughts and prayers. I read to him some of the texts people had sent from various countries. Then I prayed with him, and ended our conversation by saying, "Don't give up."

The silence on the other end of the line was unnerving. I knew Greg as a skilled leader, animated and laughing, filled with strength, resolve, and caring—and always responsive. But now he lay silent, unable to utter a word. My grief intensified. I put on one of his favorite worship songs, "Goodness of God," before I ended the call.

Before I disconnected, the nurse told me, "Your husband must have recognized your voice. He moved his hands spontaneously as you were talking, which he hadn't done yet." Then she told me that the song I had played was one she knew, so she promised to play those types of uplifting songs for Greg throughout her shift. It was such a lovely and unexpected gesture. Greg would be able to listen to worship songs even while in an ICU room and on a ventilator.

Later that day, we received news that Greg's lungs were a bit better, and in addition, he no longer needed dialysis.

I checked the family text to see if anyone had added a message. Lesley sent the perfect verse to end this trying week: "For I will restore health to you, and your wounds I will heal, declares the LORD" (Jeremiah 30:17 ESV).

I held fast to the divine hope that God would heal Greg, but whether his healing would be on earth or in heaven, I had no idea. What was God's sovereign will for us? It seemed each time I gained a flicker of hope in my husband's battle with COVID, it was soon followed by disappointment. I clung to God with all my heart. But I didn't want to be bound by a cautious hope. Instead, I wanted the power of the hope we find in Christ. No matter how heated the battle ahead would become, this was the hope I wanted to continue to cling to.

"I KNOW WHAT IT IS TO BE
POOR OR TO HAVE PLENTY,

AND I HAVE LIVED UNDER
ALL KINDS OF CONDITIONS.

I KNOW WHAT IT MEANS TO
BE FULL OR TO BE HUNGRY,

TO HAVE TOO MUCH OR TOO
LITTLE.

CHRIST GIVES ME THE
STRENGTH TO FACE
ANYTHING."

PHILIPPIANS 4:12–13 CEV

CHAPTER FOUR

Rubber Band

IT HAD BEEN EIGHT days since Greg's intubation. I sat wearily at the kitchen table that morning rehearsing the past few days. What a week it turned out to be. Yesterday was unforgettable. I was discharged from the hospital, but no one knew how I would get home. Since I'd been taken by ambulance to the hospital four days prior, my car wasn't there for me to drive myself. My son couldn't drive me because my car wouldn't allow for enough distance between us. Taxis and Ubers were out. In desperation, when my insurance representative called to check on me that day, I explained my dilemma. The agent said, "Don't worry. I'll figure something out."

Sometime later she called back to inform me that they had arranged for an ambulance to take me home, which I thought was extremely generous.

However, it soon became obvious that the hospital staff wasn't happy about this solution because ambulances were in high demand picking up critically ill COVID patients. I felt terrible about it, but there was truly no other solution.

When I was ready to leave my room, two nurses helped me into a wheelchair and escorted me, wearing heavy hazmat suits and squeaking the entire way through the bowels of the hospital. They took a route I'm sure no patient had ever seen before. When the elevator doors opened at the lowest level of the hospital building, we were bombarded by the noise from the large machinery and equipment all around us that serviced the hospital with electricity, water, and who knows what else. I felt like a menial servant who wasn't allowed to use the front entrance of a stately manor house. It was downright eerie.

Outside the hospital, the ambulance was parked in a far-away spot. The driver instructed me to sit on one specific seat only. He handed me gloves and rushed off to the driver's seat in another section of the ambulance completely separated from where I sat. When we finally arrived at my house, he swung open the door to my section of the ambulance, helped me down the steps, and hurried away. He didn't wait to see if I got safely into my house, nor did he speak to me. Although it was obvious that I was weak and moving slowly with cautious steps due to lingering body aches, he didn't seem to care.

After a surreal and stressful day—to say the least—I fell on the couch and stayed there the remainder of the afternoon and into the evening. I only exerted energy to respond to family and close friends.

Now, staring at my breakfast—a healthy one of boiled eggs and a whole-grain English muffin I'd forced myself to make—my stomach churned at the smell. I couldn't eat. Although I hadn't lost my sense of taste or smell, which was one of the symptoms of COVID, I had gained a revulsion for eggs, most meats, and anything with dairy products. The aroma of coffee also turned my stomach. I pushed the food aside and reverted to cold applesauce—something I had never cared for pre-CO-VID, but now craved. It was bizarre how this virus affected the senses.

While savoring my soothing applesauce, I turned on the news. The reporter said, "There are at least 52,976 cases of this novel coronavirus in the United States, and 704 people have now died in our country.[1]" The numbers were increasing by the day. How many would die before this pandemic ended?

I decided to call Hollie to talk about the ever-worsening CO-VID news. I was curious how things were progressing in Israel today.

Hollie agreed that the daily reports conveyed continual despair. Every day cases multiplied globally. She sensed my rising fear and understood.

We discussed the virus's effect on the world and especially on Greg. Its unstable yo-yo-like nature was puzzling. I wanted to remain strong in the Lord, but that day I felt rather weak. *Cautious hope*—was it sneaking back? I explained how I needed to brace myself in case we received more bad news today. As we talked, Hollie relayed an incredible picture the Lord had given her a few days prior.

> I was sitting in our library overlooking the snowcapped mountains in the distance, which are sometimes hard to see because of how hazy the city occasionally becomes. In my solitude, I remembered saying to the Lord, "I wish I could be like that mountain." I thought about the stories where that particular mountain was mentioned and how long that

---

1   Helen Regan, et. al. "March 25, 2020 Coronavirus News." CNN, March 26, 2020. https://edition.cnn.com/world/live-news/coronavirus-outbreak-03-25-20-intl-hnk/h_f0259e941d66f9b8e2976742eaad05c1.

mountain had been there. It had weathered every storm. It endured many wars—through death and through life. And it's the monument that stands strong and firm, immovable. I remember saying to the Lord, "I wish I was like *that*. I wish I could be strong and weather all these storms." Some time went by, and I once again found myself pondering the same thoughts in my quiet time while meditating on God. I heard the still small voice of the Lord say, "Hollie, you're not a mountain, and I never created you to be a mountain. You're looking at it all wrong and asking the wrong questions." He showed me that I was more like a rubber band. When you look at a rubber band in its natural state, its circular entity has the ability to be stretched in a way that would seem beyond its capability. The rubber band can be wrapped around something numerous times. It can stretch and bounce back to its original shape.

He encouraged me that rather than wishing I was an immovable mountain, I should accept the fact that He created me like a rubber band so that I can stretch with the times, even through hardships. I can free-fall and let go. I can let whatever is going to happen, happen, knowing that my shape will be retained, because He is the Creator, and He is my strength, and He gives me my flexibility. Maybe the reason we've been born is that we can be flexible, move, and bind something together. We can be strong like this tiny rubber band that can wrap itself tightly around something but at the same time free-fall and simultaneously bounce back and maintain its shape.

As I contemplated this powerful insight, it reminded me of Philippians 4:12–13: "I know what it is to be poor or to have plenty, and I have lived under all kinds of conditions. I know what it means to be full or to be hungry, to have too much or too little" (CEV). It is in Christ that we gain strength to face anything. I asked the Lord to help me live out those verses. I asked Him for that which I lacked—His strength. And just as He supplies us with hope no matter what the situation, I now wanted to trust Him for supernatural strength.

Greg Jr. called later that day. "I just had a meeting with Dad's critical care and pulmonary doctor. He reviewed everything with me, from Dad's head to his toes. As you know, they made many attempts these last few days to lower the ventilator's settings and eventually take Dad off the ventilator. Today, the doctor said, for the next several days, they're not going to try anything addition-ally, and they're not going to try to wean Dad off the ventilator. They're just going to be still and let Dad rest."

My first reaction was negative. Was this another way to share bad news?

Greg Jr. reassured me that wasn't necessarily the case. It was a natural stance to take for someone in his dad's condition. It could be that his body needed a break, so the advice was, "Be still."

Waiting is hard. It would be a challenge to accept being still. *Is this another stretching lesson?* Philippians 4:12–13 challenged me again to implement the words I'd read. I needed to truly exer-cise my faith in the Lord that I could accept any circumstance with His help. The Lord promised He would give me strength through any adversity. I had read it earlier that day in my go-to Psalm 91. A power-pack of verses was my daily nourishment.

When Greg Jr. came over late that afternoon, instead of meeting in the cold garage, he moved into the sunny backyard. He sat on a patio chair bundled up while I sat inside the house bundled up on a step of our indoor stairway facing the screen door into the backyard. We talked through that screen door. We agreed that the cold air in the garage would not be good for me as I wasn't yet over COVID.

Greg Jr. brought supper again, which I couldn't eat because of the smell. Would my sense of smell and my taste ever return to normal? I sure hoped so. Not happy with this, we discussed foods I needed to eat that were tolerable to ingest and vitamin supplements to take to remain healthy and regain strength. Greg Jr. said he'd make sure I got them by tomorrow.

We continued to talk about the doctor's suggestion that day to keep Greg still—not experiment on anything, not wean him from the vent, or do any other type of maneuver—simply let him be still for a few days.

My son reminded me of a Scripture in Exodus 14 that we had discussed a week ago. Interestingly, my sister, Debra, had received that Scripture from the Lord on March 17 as a prophecy regarding Greg's sickness. In that chapter, the Israelites found themselves surrounded by Pharaoh's army. Fear possessed them again along with mistrust, and they lost faith in God's provision. Facing the Red Sea meant they would surely die. Greatly distraught, they asked if they could go back into slavery—a life they at least knew. They brought their complaints and lack of faith to Moses. It always amazes me that Moses didn't react in anger or disgust, but with patient words and confident direction: "Do not be afraid. Stand firm and you will see the deliverance the LORD will bring you today. The Egyptians you see today you will never see again. The LORD will fight for you; you need only to be still" (Exodus 14:13–14).

How awesome is our Lord! He'd already given us this Scripture earlier to think about. And then today, the doctor, although totally unfamiliar with our discussions of the Scripture, used those exact words to explain their course of treatment for Greg over the next few days. Jesus, our Rescuer, is the One who fights for us so that in any circumstance that comes our way, we can turn the reins over to Him and live out Philippians 4:12–13.

As Moses had instructed the Israelites, we would also be still and watch the Lord fight this battle.

Greg remained pretty much the same the following days. However, on one of those days his kidneys began to fail, so he was back on dialysis again. He also developed three blood clots and a urinary tract infection.

On March 27, I opened Facebook to distract myself a bit. Greg Jr.'s post was the first in my newsfeed:

> Dad, you lay there in a bed, dependent on a machine to breathe for you, another machine to aid your kidneys, another to feed you, and another to drain your fluids. Basically your white flag is waving as your body has surrendered. You found your endpoint. Your physical breaking point. But you're not alone in that, Dad. I am waving mine too. It is amazing how helpless I feel. I'm now standing on the other side of the conversation for the first time. No longer am I in control of the situation, but I've had to relinquish this control to your doctors and health care providers. I'm at my end as well, Dad. I have nothing further I can do. I suppose helpless is the appropriate term.

My heart went out to my son. I could so relate. Hopelessness threatened. A part of me longed to give in to the doubt that pulled on the fringes of my mind, but I took a deep breath, grabbed hold of my faith, and made the decision to be still and watch God work.

During those days of being still, I was permitted to call and talk to Greg through the nurse's phone. I always prayed with him, read texts from friends and relatives, and ended with one of his favorite songs. The nurses thought he looked forward to my calls, but most times he didn't show much response. They attributed it to the fact that they weren't attempting to reduce his sedation to test his ability to withstand less sedation, so he wasn't waking up. He was also on increased amounts of antibiotics for the infection and other medications to dissolve the clots.

These conversations were never easy. I often found them agonizing and depressing. But we all kept on calling Greg anyway, because if there was even a small chance he could hear us and understand, we wanted him to know of our love and our prayers. We begged him to keep fighting.

My sister, Maria, was such a comfort at that time. Since she had lost her husband a few years earlier, her empathetic words were especially meaningful. She knew what it was like to see one's husband battling a devastating illness and in an unresponsive state. Her words of advice helped me walk through challenging circumstances.

As we stayed still and waited those four days, I talked with our sisters and close friends. Their kind and caring words were reassuring. My sisters continued receiving texts and emails from their many friends and acquaintances too. Prayer for Greg was growing. Many sent words of encouragement, Bible verses, and worship songs. Worship music permeated my home and filled my soul all day long. Often the timely words brought opportunities for incredible praise and prayer times—just Jesus and me.

It was my heartfelt hope that when this trial finally ended, I wouldn't lose the intimacy with God I had found through our intense alone time together. As I leaned closer to my Savior through the many ups and downs, it felt like an extended prayer retreat. I didn't want it to become merely a distant memory, but a lifetime closeness with my Best Friend.

Greg Jr. flew back to San Diego a day later, on March 28. It was a difficult decision for him, but the regulations and restrictions of plane travel had increased. Cancellations all over the United States and around the world were on the rise daily. *Quarantine* and *isolation* were the operative terms for people in most countries.

Since he could no longer be in the hospital to observe his dad through his COVID ICU room window and could only confer with doctors and staff by phone and text, it made perfect sense for him to return to San Diego. We all agreed the safest place for him was with Lesley and their four children. He needed to fly home before it became impossible to do so.

Improvement in my health was slow, but I was well taken care of since friends continually dropped off food at my doorstep. Our primary care doctor called every few days to check on me. Even though my children couldn't be with me, I would be okay.

That same day, Sarah, the nurse who attended to Greg the most, called and said that they were back to reducing the sedation. She thought, before he became anxious from reducing the sedation, which had been his pattern, this might be a good time to ask him some questions.

When she had asked him if he wanted to talk to me, he squeezed her hand.

She was so encouraged that he responded with such certainty, she immediately called me. So, once again I talked with him as if I was right there in that room—a room I had never seen in person. I spoke as though he might answer, but the absence of his audible voice pierced me like the first time. I could only hope that he could hear the voices of his family and that it filled the emptiness he might be feeling, especially since none of us could sit beside him, hold his hand, or have any physical contact with him.

Sarah's cheery voice spoke into the receiver. "He listened intently as you spoke. I really do believe he hears you, and I think he knows when you and the family call him. I know you must be discouraged, but don't be. We are all taking this one day at a time. We're all hoping this time he will adjust to the lower vent settings and be weaned from the vent entirely."

I was glad that the medical team chose to begin the sedation withdrawal trials once again. I prayed they would be successful in weaning him off the vent, and he could finally breathe on his own without assistance from the machine that was keeping him alive.

After dinner, Sarah called and said he became extremely anxious again as they lowered his sedation, so they had to raise the sedation level once more.

Today had not been a successful attempt. Disappointment and cautious hope tried once again to reside in my heart.

As I lay in bed that night, I reminisced about my day, especially my call with Greg, who had been unresponsive. Tears filled my eyes. He needed a miracle. It wasn't the first time we needed God to intervene for us in our 49-year marriage. Instead of counting sheep to help me fall asleep, I counted the times the Lord had met our needs since 1971 when we were married.

After our junior year at Central Bible College (CBC), we got married. I went to CBC part-time and worked part-time at a preschool. Greg went to school full-time and worked part-time at a meat market. We didn't have much money to live on after we paid our few bills and especially our school bill. Food was the last priority. By the end of the month, we quite often had to live on peanut butter sandwiches, potato soup, and onion soup.

One Sunday morning after church in 1972, although we had managed to pay all the bills for that month, we dreaded going home to face another round of potato soup. It was the only thing left to eat in our house. We knew better than to ask our parents for extra money. After all, they had suggested we wait until after graduation to marry, but since we had already dated for four years and refused to wait any longer, they gave us their blessing and we married.

Before the first spoonful reached our mouths, the doorbell rang. We hurried to the door, but no one was there. On the front step sat three bags of groceries. A car we didn't recognize zoomed away as we stood staring after it. We carried the bags to the counter, peeked inside, and found a card from our Sunday school class. I opened it and read it to Greg, "We wanted to bless you today. Enjoy."

Our hearts leaped with excitement as we pulled out item after item of delicious foods we hadn't tasted in weeks—fresh fruits of all kinds, milk, cereals, pancake mix, maple syrup, cookies, and so much more. Tears ran down our faces as we praised God.

We pushed the soup aside and began to devour the tasty morsels generously given to us by our church family.

We hadn't told anyone how poor we were. Our Sunday school class had no way of knowing. We'd determined to live according to Philippians 4:12–13: "I have learned the secret to being content in any and every situation, whether well fed or hungry, whether living in plenty or in want. I can do all this through him who gives me strength."

That day we understood that although God had given us strength to endure during our time of need, He also provides beyond our need and blesses us abundantly. He stretches us like rubber bands to teach us greater lessons. The bags of groceries felt like hugs from our Lord. He was always aware of our needs. Nothing was hidden from Him. But at the right time, He chose to bless us beyond our expectations.

As I recalled that precious incident from years ago, it brought a smile to my face. God was fully aware of Greg's urgent need today. He was in charge. Perhaps the Lord was allowing us to wait so He could stretch our family to hold on, not give up, and continue to trust Him.

On the morning of March 29, Greg Jr. gave us an update on his dad. Dialysis was initiated again, and his lung x-rays didn't look good. Although we were used to the yo-yo routine, over time the instability of his condition increased our doubts and questions. I asked Greg Jr., "What does this really mean?" I wanted to know what the timeline was for COVID to run its course in a patient as sick as his dad.

He answered, "No one knows. We could be nearing the end of the need for the ventilator, or we could still be at the beginning or the middle of it. This disease is only predictable in the sense that each day will be different. The only constant in Dad's health is change."

It seemed the answer was that there were no straightforward answers. No one really knew much about COVID and its prognosis patterns. We were back to the only answer we had so far: to watch and be still.

Later that day I received a text from our friend, Mark, a pastor in Bowie, Maryland, who is like a brother to Greg. From the start of Greg's illness, Mark faithfully texted twice a day, often sending verses and songs. Today Mark sent a prayer along with Psalm 27:1: "You, Lord, are the light that keeps me safe. I am not afraid of anyone. You protect me, and I have no fears" (CEV).

I understood what the Lord was driving home these last few days. No matter what state we find ourselves in, no matter how Greg's illness fared, our Lord never changes. He's all about rescuing us, fighting for us, protecting us, and stretching us to maintain consistent trust in Him as He pours His strength into us to keep us pressing on in any circumstance.

My grandson, Alec, seemed to understand this. COVID's demands were difficult for everyone, even in Israel. Jason, on returning home from the States, had to quarantine for two weeks away from his family, so he stayed in an apartment below theirs. Hollie would bring him food by his doorstep, and they would converse six feet apart as she sat on a stair step, and he remained in the doorway to his temporary downstairs apartment. The children had school through Zoom in the Hebrew language. Each had to go to a separate space in their home with their computer and attend classes all day. This caused unbelievable stress for the kids and their parents.

It was one of those days for Hollie when the report on her dad was negative and the distance between us as a family was disconcerting. Hollie told me, "I was vacuuming while Alec was in the living room playing a video game. I started bawling, thinking about Dad. Alec turned around and heard me crying. Looking at me with caring eyes, he said, 'Mom, turn the vacuum off.' I turned it off. Tears continued to flow down my face. Alec looked at me with a calm and confident expression. Absolute peace covered him, and he said, 'Mom, Papa's gonna be okay. Papa's gonna live. Did you hear me? He's going to live, Mom.'"

Hollie said later, "I've held onto that. There were moments when we weren't sure, but Alec was so convinced. It was like the Holy Spirit spoke right through him with authority. But more than that—a gentle but firm assurance was coupled with that authority."

The knowledge that twelve-year-old Alec made it a priority to seek Jesus for his papa's illness and allowed the Holy Spirit to speak through him emphasized that our grandchildren weren't angry with God for Greg's stricken condition. They knew to go to God for answers and for healing.

Two days later I felt stronger, although I still needed to rest and take naps. I continued to struggle with horrid smells and strange tastes, but had noticeable improvement. The sun was out, and I longed to go outside for a few minutes to smell the fresh air and feel the rays of the sun on my face. I walked to my mailbox ten yards from my house and found four notes from my San Diego grandkids. My heart felt light as I sat down to read them, wearing the biggest smile ever.

> Nonni,
> I miss you so much! These times can be very hard, out of our control, and hard to manage. You are strong, hard-working, and an amazing grandmother. Papa is out of our control but is 100% in God's. So I am okay with that. I've been reading Psalm 62:8. God can handle everything, and we can pour our hearts out to Him always. I'm so glad that you have overcome this sickness! I

love you so so so much! I miss you and can't wait to see you when this is all over!
Love you!
Emery (15)

Dear Nonni,
I love you sooooo much and can't imagine what you are going through. I wish that all of us could be there with you! Hoping that we get to see you soon! Love you so much.
Grey (13)
P.S. And feel free to text whenever. I'm always here. I also wrote an essay for school that I am sending for you to read. The topic is "Biblical Justice."

Dear Nonni,
I love you so, so much. I have been praying for you guys every day. I always love when you guys bicker at the table when we are playing Monopoly. Love you to death.
Lincoln (12)

Dear Nonni,
I pray for you and Papa to feel better. I hope you will know that everything God has under control. We have been praying for you and Papa every day. You guys are the best Nonni and Papa. You should know that Papa is going to be with you every day. I pray that Papa gets better and will come back home to you. You should never be scared because God knows everything. We love you guys so much and we are praying for you two.
Sincerely,
Ainslee (9)

I read those precious notes over and over, relishing their sincerity. It was an expression of their individual personalities. I thanked God for each of them. They were a life-giving support system. And their faith in God and prayer was obvious, which was music to this nonni's heart.

The ache in my heart to see my eight grandkids and have them near intensified as each one continued to express their strong belief that their papa would be healed from this devastating pandemic attack.

My thoughts were interrupted when I received a voice message from Greg Jr., requesting we have a family call as soon as possible. His voice sounded serious. Our many phone conversations since Greg's illness had been filled with a variety of emotions, always dependent on Greg's current condition. Sometimes the tone was solemn, other times relaxed. There were times we shared raw emotion, both good and bad. We even shared a chuckle or two. Perhaps I was simply reading something into his voice, since receiving bad news was part of our roller coaster battle with COVID.

Once we were all connected to our family call, Greg Jr. got right to the point. "As you know, Dad has been on a ventilator for fifteen days now. With each day that passes, the prognosis worsens. He's been placed on dialysis again to maintain his kidney function and keep his lungs dry."

Greg Jr. paused a moment, and I braced myself for whatever would follow.

"The fact is his lungs are starting to fail. He struggles to breathe and feels the need to breathe forty to fifty times per minute. That's kind of like sprinting in the middle of a marathon. So, the doctor had to increase his sedation and let the ventilator work for Dad's lungs."

I rubbed my forehead. It was as I had suspected; the news was disheartening. "Do they have a plan?" I choked out.

Greg Jr. cleared his throat. "Well, we have all been praying for wisdom for the doctors and medical staff. And today Dad's ICU doctors called a meeting with me because they're unsure of what the next step should be. They've done all they can. They mentioned the potential of a transfer."

"What kind of transfer?" Jason asked.

"They brought up a tertiary care facility. Through a series of phone calls, Dad was accepted at Barnes-Jewish Hospital in St. Louis. I believe God answered our prayers and gave wisdom to the doctors involved in Dad's care. They found a bed for him in the COVID ICU. It's a miracle that the Critical COVID ICU Unit at Barnes-Jewish Hospital agreed, because transferring a COVID patient is an unknown entity. It increases risk to the healthcare workers who make the transfer. I believe God answered our prayers."

"So, they're going to move him to St. Louis?" I tried to wrap my mind around the fact that my husband would be transported so far away from our hometown and . . . from me, but if it helped him. . . .

"Well, here's the thing. We need to debate this decision. There is a risk that something will go wrong even in the transfer, and there's no guarantee that if Dad makes it to Barnes-Jewish Hospital, he will survive. But I think it's a risk worth taking."

"How much of a risk would it be to transport him?" I asked with growing concern.

"Fact is, with all he's hooked up to, and already in very serious condition, the risk is something to consider. They have to move him with the ventilator and take him off the dialysis machine. There are lots of things that can go wrong on this transport. We know how he's still fighting this unstable virus, has been two weeks on the ventilator, has pulmonary failure issues, and has kidney failure for which he needs dialysis. He has blood clots in his arms and legs, cardiac complications from experimental medications, bedsores, gastrointestinal infection, and urinary tract infection. If that isn't enough, he has bilateral secondary pneumonia, has had sepsis, and so many other serious issues."

"Oh . . . " I moaned. Just hearing the list made my stomach turn. *Oh, Greg. . . .*

"But the doctors believe there's a chance Dad can still survive this, right?" Hollie asked.

"Let's put it this way." Greg Jr. paused for a moment. "The ICU doctors at Mercy have asked about Dad's advance directive. They are considering potentially withdrawing care. You know what that means."

Everyone stayed silent.

Greg Jr. continued. "But the doctors spoke highly of the COVID-19 protocol at Barnes-Jewish Hospital and would like to give Dad a chance at recovery there. But we have to understand that he might not survive the trip. And we must face reality too. Mom, as hard as this is for all of us, I care that you really understand and face the possibility that Dad might die. Even if he survives the trip, he might still die at Barnes-Jewish Hospital. There is no promise that they can save his life. And even if he comes off the ventilator, we must take into account the possible prognosis of life-altering complications."

Hollie spoke in a comforting voice. "That's why weighing the risks is so important, Mom. Do we want to take that risk?"

The silence was deafening as we processed this candid and heart-wrenching information.

I finally spoke up. "Sounds to me that if he stays here, he will most likely die. However, even though there is a high risk he won't make it if he's transported to Barnes-Jewish Hospital, if he does make it, he will at least have a chance, however small, that his life might be saved. If there's a chance that Dad might recover at Barnes-Jewish Hospital, then that's the choice we'll make. As much as the vigilant and skilled doctors at Mercy Hospital have done, it sounds like options are running out here. As far as Dad facing any disability after so long on a ventilator, the flip side is he may fully recover. I think we have to give him that chance."

"I agree," Hollie said.

"What we are doing is surrendering this all to God," Lesley said. "Surrender is not the same as giving up. Surrender is saying, 'I can't control this.' And if Dad's life hinges on the fact that we need to be in control of this situation, then we're ultimately setting ourselves up for failure. So, we will surrender to God and not lose hope."

"I also want to remind us all," Jason pointed out, "that Dad spent his life serving the Lord. He loves God with all his heart. So, the greatest risk for us is losing him, but he would immediately be in eternity with God. Dad has nothing to lose. But if there's a chance that this move will allow him to stay longer here with us, I agree with everyone—it's a risk worth taking."

"I think so, too. But Mom . . . " Greg Jr. pleaded, "you need to be prepared that Dad might die. There is a good chance he won't make it." I heard the slightest quiver in his voice as he said, "Please, we need you to understand that."

It felt as though I were being stretched to my breaking point, but our options were limited and without guarantees. Either I trusted God, or I didn't.

"I do," I whispered as the stinging pain of those words choked me. I cleared my throat. "How about we pray together right now for God's hand to be on this transfer? We don't want to undertake this without asking for His blessing. It is obvious that only with prayer can it be successful."

> **"Surrender is not the same as giving up. Surrender is saying 'I can't control this.'"**

When we finished, Hollie spoke in a sober but confident tone. "It's time to release Dad. Release him from Mercy Hospital and release him once again into God's hands as we face this next step."

"HE HAS DELIVERED US FROM
SUCH A DEADLY PERIL,

AND HE WILL DELIVER US AGAIN.

ON HIM WE HAVE SET OUR HOPE
THAT HE WILL

CONTINUE TO DELIVER US,

AS YOU HELP US BY YOUR
PRAYERS.

THEN MANY WILL GIVE THANKS
ON OUR BEHALF

FOR THE GRACIOUS FAVOR
GRANTED US

IN ANSWER TO THE PRAYERS OF
MANY."

2 CORINTHIANS 1:10–11 NIV

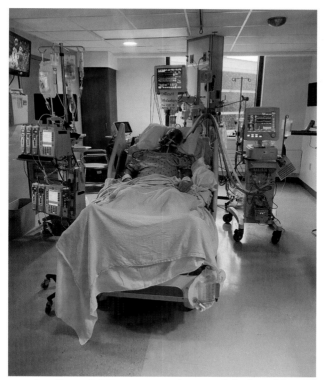

Greg, the first COVID-19 patient at his local hospital to go on a ventilator.

March 23—Greg Jr. delivers groceries to Mom.

Greg Jr., Lesley, Emery, Greyson, Lincoln, and Ainslee

#rallyhope post generated a tsunami of prayer partners.

April 4—Hollie, Jason, and children meeting
Mom in the garage.

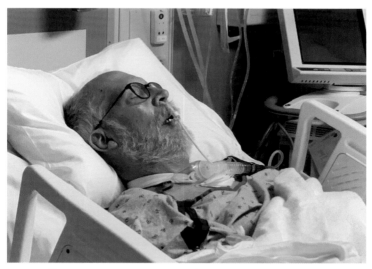

April 22–May 6—Greg at the transitional hospital
in Springfield, Missouri.

Sandie and family visiting Greg through the hospital window in Springfield.

May 13—Hollie's first in-person visit with her dad at the in-patient rehabilitation hospital.

May 17—The grandchildren get ready for Papa's homecoming after sixty days in four different hospitals.

May 17—Welcome Home Papa!
Back row: Hollie, Audrey, Jason, Ava.
Front row: Aris, Papa, Alec.

May 27—Greg Jr. and Greg.

May 30—Papa and family with #rallyhope hats.

#rallyhope

Mom, you must face *the possibility that Dad might die.* I couldn't get those words out of my mind. Over the past two weeks, through the continual ups and downs of Greg's critical condition, of course I understood he could die. After all, the day he was admitted to the hospital, he had been given a ten percent chance of living through the night. For some reason, I didn't dwell on that. I tried to put it out of my mind. I guess I just didn't let it take root in my heart after that first night of survival. Whenever those thoughts tried to sneak in, I pushed them aside. But I now realized I hadn't resolved this issue.

The blunt statement nagged at me. Nothing could distract me away from the question. Had I settled it? One thing was certain. I could no longer avoid the possibility of such an outcome.

As I stared out the window into the cold, pitch-dark night, the harsh reality that Greg might die gripped me.

Greg was in flight. Would he die during this short transport? I felt nauseated and anxious. God knew my thoughts, but that wasn't enough at the moment. I paced around the room and cried out loud to the Lord. "I've trusted You all my life. You're the One who brought us through so many difficulties. I know You're here now in this dark hour too. I may not feel You, but I trust Your faithfulness. You are my solid rock. You are my fortress. Oh, Lord, I need You now more than ever."

In faith, I clung to this truth as my mind reached back to experiences where Jesus had clearly made a way for us when no other way was visible. One incident came to the forefront.

In January 1999, Greg was Europe Regional Director for AGWM. He and the AGWM videographer, Tim, took a ministry trip to Serbia and Kosovo even though fighting had already begun in this civil war. Their purpose was to visit the struggling churches in both provinces and to take videos of the awesome revival occurring in Leskovac, Serbia, among the Roma (gypsies), a marginalized group of people.

After a few days of meetings with pastors in Beograd, Serbia, Greg and Tim made their way to Leskovac, accompanied by a Serbian friend, Milan, who was a lawyer.

This was on a Sunday night. The tiny church with no windows was packed to capacity. Women and children sat on one side and men on the other. There were so many men in that service that they had to remove all the seats to allow for standing room only. The men stood shoulder to shoulder throughout the entire service.

The first service was lively and filled with God's presence. Due to the crowd, there was no room for an altar where people could come forward for salvation and healing. Instead, they had to raise their hands high to be recognized and then meet with the elders later.

Greg and Tim were sweating profusely in their mandatory sports jackets. How would they survive the second service in this unrelenting heat?

They stared in amazement as an even larger crowd of people squeezed inside the small, windowless building. The heat, however, could not hold back the power of God, and many received Christ for the first time in that service.

Four young men who were new believers from a neighboring village came to the second service. They had brought their drug-addicted friend and actually carried him from the hospital, where he had been lying on his death bed. He had sniffed so much glue that he had destroyed his throat and couldn't eat, drink, or swallow. The hospital fed him intravenously. His four friends knew that only Jesus could deliver him. They got permission from the hospital to take their dying friend out for just a few hours to go to church. Before the service ended, that young addict had been radically saved and healed. Later, we heard that the news of his miraculous healing brought revival to his small town. Just like the woman at the well after her encounter with Jesus (John 4:1–30), the young man couldn't stop talking about his Healer, who had delivered him and given him a new life.

The day after that service, Greg, Tim, and Milan drove 155 miles to Pristina, Kosovo, where they intended to stop briefly at a pastor friend's house for refreshments. Their end goal that day was Beograd, Serbia. They were warned not to attempt crossing the border at night because of the Serbian militia, who were increasing in number and could stop cars randomly and make unreasonable and dangerous demands. Unfortunately, they left much later than planned and faced darkness not far into their trip.

Shortly after they crossed the Serbian border, a roadblock appeared out of nowhere. They were forced to slow down and then stop.

Milan rattled off instructions to Greg and Tim in his broken English. "When the militia come to our car, don't say a word!" To Tim, seated in the back seat, he urgently instructed, "Hide the video camera between your legs." As they watched, the militiaman began walking in their direction. Milan blurted, "Only let *me* do the talking."

Greg became extremely alarmed, not only because of Milan's obvious fear, but because the militia soldier nearing their car carried a Kalashnikov assault rifle.

When the soldier came to the driver's side, Greg rolled down his window in cooperation.

Immediately the rifle was pushed into his chest, and a battle of Serbian words were volleyed between the militia soldier and Milan. Every time the lawyer's voice rose, the soldier pushed the rifle deeper into Greg's chest. With every movement of the weapon, fear multiplied. Perhaps this was it. This was how he was going to die. As he prayed for God to deliver them, he was certain Tim joined him in silent prayer. Was their death imminent?

After a few more minutes of intense and boisterous conversation between Milan and the militia soldier, the man pulled his gun away from Greg's chest with a rough and abrupt shift, waved his hand in what seemed like great disgust, and motioned them to move on.

When they were a few miles past the roadblock, all three men began praising the Lord with loud voices. They thanked Him for delivering them from what could have been horrendous bloodshed.

Milan explained to Greg and Tim what his conversation with the militia soldier had been about. In essence, he told the militiaman that he was a Serbian lawyer from Beograd and the two men with him were visiting friends. He explained that his friends were simply driving back to his home in Beograd with him.

Since Serbia was not on good terms with the United States, if the militia had known Milan's guests were from the USA, the entire incident could have ended much differently.

Indeed, Jesus had intervened. Greg, Tim, and Milan's lives had hung in the balance, but Jesus protected them from harm.

Jesus was never late in His intervention. Recalling this incident assured me that the Lord would not be late in taking hold of Greg's future this time either.

I poured out my heart to God and expressed my fears, but also thanked Him for His faithfulness all through the years . . . over and over. My words became calmer as His presence filled my living room, and I found the strength to surrender it all to Him. "Dear God, I release Greg to You. I want only Your will for him. If this is the time when You are calling him to enter heaven and leave his earthly home, leave his family, his calling,

I surrender it all to You. I trust You. And I love You. I will give You praise whatever You choose to do."

Indescribable peace poured over me. It was a peace that brought rest and confidence at the same time. The Lord was here. I couldn't see Him, but His presence was as close as a person sitting right beside me. In that moment I understood that the Lord would walk with me and commune with me no matter what the future would bring. I didn't want to ever leave His holy presence. I yearned for this intimacy with Him. My soul welled up with thanksgiving, and I promised the Lord, "If You take him home, I will rejoice; and if You heal him, I will rejoice, but in either case, I promise to declare Your goodness, Your power, and Your miraculous nature. I'll proclaim it loudly until You take me home."

After all that intense praying, crying, and with ongoing weakness from COVID, I was exhausted. However, the agony that had crippled my spirit was gone, replaced with an assurance that I no longer had to wrestle with "cautious hope" regardless of how the situation would turn out. The Lord never changes. God is the only supplier of everlasting hope—always! He is our hope. "Those who hope in the LORD will renew their strength" (Isaiah 40:31).

I looked at the clock. After 12 a.m. It was April 1. One of the nurses who accompanied Greg in the helicopter had promised to call when they landed at Barnes-Jewish Hospital. Even though I knew his chance of survival was minimal during this flight, the peace God gave me delivered me from my former panicked reaction. I trusted Him. If the Lord could save Greg from likely death by a militiaman with an assault rifle in Serbia, He could just as easily protect him on a flight to St. Louis, despite all the needed hookups and Greg's critical state. Hadn't God proved over and over that nothing is too difficult for Him?

It was a little past one o'clock in the morning when the nurse called. Greg had made it safely to St. Louis. They were busy moving him into his room. Another miracle!

He was now in a new place I'd never seen before. The thought was disquieting. Our family had to trust his new medical team and hospital to care for the man we loved and couldn't imagine living without. But we had prayed for wisdom as a family, and the Lord answered with the miracle of a room for Greg at Barnes-Jewish Hospital. As Hollie had said, "It's time to release Dad. Release him from Mercy Hospital and release him into God's hands."

Earlier that evening, while Greg was in flight, Hollie and Jason decided it was time to come to Springfield since her dad's condition was considered "touch and go" and growing more urgent every day. Also, announcements were made each day of more countries around the world closing airports and not allowing visitors in or out. They needed to act fast and make their plans to leave Israel as soon as possible, and they had to pack for what would probably be a lengthy stay.

Their flight was booked for April 4, the last flight out of Israel to New York until there was more clarity about the future of the pandemic.

When Hollie told me the news, I was surprised it would be possible for them to come home. I had refused to put pressure on them to make such a decision despite her dad's illness, especially during this crazy time. But the news filled me with incredible joy. I hated the reason that necessitated this decision, but loved that they would be here with me through the rest of this journey.

Since I was still not allowed out of quarantine, they planned to spend a week at an Airbnb. When I was finally released from quarantine, they would move in with me. They didn't bother with return tickets since it was impossible to predict when they'd be allowed back into Israel. It took a lot of courage, love, and sacrifice for them to make this trip during this uncertain pandemic.

I reflected on the day as I lay in bed that night, my heart filled with gratitude. Greg had made it safely to Barnes-Jewish Hospital, and Hollie, Jason, and the kids would be here soon.

I picked up my phone to see if Greg Jr. had posted an update on Facebook. I began reading his latest post.

"Hope means hoping when things are hopeless, or it is no virtue at all. . . . As long as matters are really hopeful, hope is mere flattery or platitude; it is only when everything is hopeless that hope begins to be a strength." G.K. Chesterton.

In baseball, Chesterton's quote is akin to being down by 3 in the bottom of the ninth inning, 2 outs, bases loaded, and the final batter takes the plate. The crowd in desperation makes one more declaration of hope. The final batter. The only hope of victory. Everyone in the stands rotates their hats 180 degrees and flips them inside out, signifying the hope and faith placed in the last batter. It is in this moment that "hope begins to be a strength."

Growing up, every four years our family would return to the USA from Austria for Dad (and the rest of us) to visit churches around the country in an effort to share our story and raise financial support. This was critical to our ability to spend another 4 years overseas. We called this year a furlough. What this would mean for Hollie and me is that we got to sit through 1000s of church services, listening to worship, pastors introducing our family, and then my dad usually preaching a sermon . . . the same sermon . . . Sunday morning, Sunday evening, and Wednesday evening . . . repeat . . . for a year!!! Needless to say, after this year was over we could have preached and Dad could have sat in the pew and listened to us. Looking back, Dad preached one of my favorite sermons of all time on hope. I was 6 years old . . . or 10 . . . (I forget which furlough it was). As a child, however, sitting through so many services could get challenging, particularly for an energetic little boy. For me, listening to his sermon was like driving across the country. At some point you get so bored you start counting how many green cars you pass on the highway. Please time, pass by! So I remember Hollie and me playing a game and counting how many times dad would say the word "hope." 136. I remember, 136x!!!

Looking back it makes sense. Dad was gripped, feeling as if he was at the end of his ability to share God's story of redemption and reconciliation. Hope is literally what sustained my father. Hope was the reason he would never give up on his calling in Austria. Hope is why he never gave up on his family, his friends, and ultimately his faith.

G.K. Chesterton understood the concept of hope, and no doubt my father is reliving his sermon from so many years ago. So Dad, take that Buckeyes hat, put it in the #rallyhope position and join me and 1000x1000 prayers that are being lifted on behalf of so many affected by COVID-19, and BEAT this virus!

I felt so inspired by Greg Jr.'s words that I was turning my imaginary hat in bed in the #rallyhope position and joining my family of prayer partners all over the world in prayer for Greg and the multitude of others in dire need from COVID. I so wished Greg knew the intense love of his children who rallied hope for their very ill father that day, each one in a significant way—Hollie and family by deciding to travel home on the last flight during this pandemic and Greg by posting such an in-spiring message to our thousands of prayer partners around the globe.

Greg Jr.'s #rallyhope post blew up with thousands of re-sponses. A multitude of people posted selfies, hats turned in the #rallyhope position, and promised to support us in prayer. A global choir of voices interceded for Greg's healing and recov-ery as well as for the worldwide victims of COVID during this pandemic.

Late in the evening on April 2, I searched the internet for up-dates on the coronavirus. *More than 215,000 people have been diag-nosed with COVID-19 in the United States, according to Johns Hopkins University late Wednesday night. More than 5,000 people have died from the disease across the country.*[1] With how quickly the death toll was rising, how many more would die this week? Would Greg be next?

The news became gloomier by the day. Weddings had to be limited to close family and be conducted outdoors. All gather-ings were highly discouraged. Funeral services were prohibit-ed, and restaurants and movie theaters were closed. Travel was limited, professional sports were canceled, and churches were made to close their doors, most converting to online options. Many businesses expected their employees to work online

1   CBS News. "Coronavirus Updates from April 1, 2020." CBS News, April 2, 2020. https://www.cbsnews.com/live-updates/coronavirus-pan-demic-covid-19-latest-news-2020-04-01/.

from home and conduct meetings through Zoom. Schools had closed, and most operated through Zoom calls with students. Homeschooling was suddenly accepted by everyone. Many small businesses such as barbershops and hair salons closed indefinitely. Everyone had to wear masks. Never could any of us have imagined such mandates accepted in the United States and around the world by the public at large.

Zoom meetings had become the norm. Drive-by celebrations became popular, where people slowly drove by the celebrant's house while yard signs with balloons blowing in the breeze proclaimed "Happy Birthday" or whatever the occasion being celebrated. People in cars left gifts at the curbside and waved at their friends or family who stood on their front lawn, smiling and thanking them for driving by, always maintaining social distance. What once could only be found in dystopian fiction had become our reality.

For those with happy home lives, this wasn't such a bad thing. Everyone got to hang out together, sort of a vacation or, more accurately, a staycation. Neighbors who had been too busy before now waved at one another and spent time chatting while maintaining the mandatory six-foot distance. These were the perfect scenarios. Unfortunately, that wasn't everyone's life. Many who lived in dysfunctional or abusive homes lost the reprieve they used to find at school or work. For those who lived alone, isolation became a place of extreme loneliness.

I continued reading comments people posted on Greg Jr.'s Facebook page. Steve, from a San Diego-based spine company, posted that he wanted to express complete outpouring of support for Greg Jr. and our family. He said that #rallyhope went viral at the company. His comment included a picture of over fifty employees with their hats turned in support of #rallyhope.

A worker in Thailand shared: *I posted a photo of you online and got a ton of response from Bh-tanese friends all saying they are praying for you. . . . It shows that your reach has extended to every country of the world!*

A close friend from St. Louis wrote: *Setting up a 24-hour prayer vigil for Greg Mundis.*

Our long-time friends in Austria texted: *Greetings from our whole Pentecostal family in Austria. Many of our leaders remember the great ministry of Greg and Sandie in Austria over the many years. We are in deep friendship with you. . . . "Commit your way to the Lord; trust him, and he will act. He will bring forth your righteousness as the light, and your justice as the noonday. Be still before the Lord and wait patiently for him" (Psalm 37:5–7 ESV). Blessings!*

I read comment after comment, the same sentiments of encouragement and support.

I had to stop reading. Tears clouded my eyes as more streamed down my face. Although we were forced to isolate ourselves from each other physically, it seemed we had managed to gather for the combined purpose of seeing Greg and countless others healed. We were separated by distance, but united in zeal. Literally thousands of people prayed around the clock and around the world. Hundreds of churches promised corporate prayer for Greg; the vast majority of their congregants didn't know him personally.

After the #rallyhope post, I couldn't keep up with all the comments, songs, and Bible verses that were posted daily. Despite all this amazing support, Greg's condition did *not* improve. Instead, he developed a fungal infection because of the many antibiotics. Another day went by, and the ventilator settings remained the same. Greg wasn't getting better.

Barnes-Jewish Hospital was doing the best they knew how for someone in Greg's condition, but would it be enough? Perhaps once COVID ran its course through Greg's body, he would begin to heal. I wanted to believe for a good outcome, but the evidence staring me in the face wasn't encouraging.

A cloud of heaviness settled over me that rainy, gloomy day. Would Hollie and her family arrive home to a funeral? Was *this* God's plan for our family—to grieve together?

Even with such weighty thoughts, I felt Jesus near. I listened to some of my favorite worship songs that people had sent these past several days. As I listened to "Waymaker," the lyrics reached into the depth of my soul and I meditated on the facts that *He will always make a way. He always keeps His promises. He is our Light in the darkest hours. And even when we don't see or feel He is intervening—He is. He simply never stops!* Listening to the song and singing the words over and over lifted the cloud and gave me peace. I fell asleep and dreamt an unforgettable dream:

A man with a flowing, long white robe walked into Greg's room at the hospital. It was Jesus. I recognized Him immediately, although I only saw His back. As I watched in amazement, He climbed onto the bed and covered Greg with His sparkling robe. I couldn't see Greg's body at all. Jesus breathed into Greg's mouth, and I heard the words from Ezekiel 37:5: "I will make breath enter you, and you will come to life."

When I awoke, the memory of the dream filled my mind. The words played in my thoughts repeatedly. Jesus was in control, and He would breathe new life into Greg's damaged lungs and body. Jesus was still the One in control, not the virus. Again, I remembered the words in Psalm 91: "His huge outstretched arms protect you. Under them you are perfectly safe" (MSG).

Jesus was still the One in control, not the virus.

I didn't know when this miracle would take place. I instinctively knew it wouldn't be immediate. I had to hold on in faith that the Lord was working, and His timing would be perfect. We would continue to watch, pray, wait, and see what God would do.

As Hollie told me of her flight to Springfield, Missouri, with Jason, their four children, and their feisty dog, Leo, on April 4, I listened with rapt attention and shook my head in amazement. How had life suddenly become so bizarre?

They had boarded a massive, 250-seat jet in Tel Aviv, but only twenty passengers were on board. There was no problem with social distancing on that flight, but masks were still mandatory. Once they arrived in New York, their flight to Denver had been canceled. Soon after, they discovered that their flight from Denver to Springfield had also been canceled. An alternative option was given—a flight to St. Louis. Perfect. They would arrive much earlier than originally planned.

Jason and Hollie decided to rent a car in St. Louis and drive the three hours to Springfield. Once the family was settled in the car and were on the road to their final destination, Jason surprised them by taking a detour and driving directly to Barnes-Jewish Hospital. They pulled into one of the parking lots overlooking the massive structure, but they had no idea where the COVID ICU Unit was located. It didn't matter. They couldn't enter the hospital anyway.

Hollie gazed up at the rooftop of the hospital since that's where the helicopter must have landed only a few days ago. It felt strange not to be allowed to visit her dad when she was so close to him. Overwhelmed with emotion, she lifted her arms and praised God that her dad had remained alive through their journey home. Hollie's family joined their voices to hers.

Jason prayed a prayer that was recorded, and it still gives me goose bumps when I listen to it. How prophetic it had been.

Although Hollie couldn't physically be with her dad in his room, she was certainly closer than she'd been a day ago in Israel. For that, she was grateful.

When they arrived in Springfield, before their family headed to the Airbnb rental, they stopped at my house. Bright sunshine lit the sky as they pulled into our driveway that afternoon. My heart raced, filled with delight, as I watched them climb out of the car.

The six-foot-distance requirement was pure torture to a woman who hadn't seen her children and grandchildren for such a long time. I longed to pull each one of them into a great big bear hug and give them kisses. But the fear of this virus passing to any of them held me in check.

We gathered in the garage and settled into chairs at a proper distance. It required great restraint to stay away from my grandchildren the entire time we chatted. Seven months had passed since I'd last seen them. With all that had transpired since Greg became ill two-and-a-half weeks ago, the longing to have them near had intensified. It was almost too much to bear.

Once Hollie's family settled into their rental house, the kids' school had to resume on Zoom. The eight-hour time difference proved to be a great challenge. Hollie had a full-time job coordinating school schedules, workspaces, and homework. It was all done in Hebrew, and the children went to four different schools. Complicated doesn't begin to describe it. However, it was a profound comfort and blessing to have Hollie and her family in Springfield.

We received wonderful news about Greg the same day that Hollie's family moved into their rental house. Greg had finally tested negative for COVID. Another reason to celebrate.

We celebrated the smallest victory in a battle that offered such sparse hope. After a family call with my children, we felt such intense joy over this bit of positive news that each of my children celebrated with their children in their respective homes. Although I was alone, I also celebrated. I pulled out a small container of ice cream from my freezer that I'd been saving for a special occasion. *This* was special. I had a party of thanksgiving with the Lord while I enjoyed some delicious rocky road ice cream that I could finally stomach.

However, the next few days after Hollie's arrival in Springfield, Greg's condition continued the same see-saw pattern we'd seen before. With every negative report, I remembered my dream. Jesus was working, whether we could see the progress or not, and we held on to that. This was the time to be patient. We continued to rally hope through prayer.

The doctors considered the important next step—a tracheostomy. The goal was to remove the ventilator tube from his mouth, since it had become increasingly bothersome, and administer it through a tracheotomy. This would require opening a direct airway through an incision in his neck and inserting a tube. The procedure is called a tracheostomy. When accomplished, they hoped to lessen Greg's sedation from the ventilator, allowing him to wake up more oriented so he could participate in breathing with the vent instead of fighting against it. Once he could do this and maintain the oxygen at an appropriate level, they would consider weaning Greg off the ventilator and getting rid of the tube.

It sounded easy, but it wasn't.

Greg Jr. explained to the family that the doctors were hesitant about this procedure because COVID had turned protocol on its head. "When you place a tracheostomy, you could potentially aerosolize the virus and place everyone in the room at risk. The result is a circular problem that leads to prolonged intubation."

It was like watching an awkward couple stumble through a slow dance. This dance was performed by a skilled medical team and Greg. My family and I were the spectators. Would they learn to dance in sync? How long would we have to watch with bated breath, hearts uneasy?

We had no control over any of this. The decisions were not ours to make. We participated from our audience seats by praying, and praying again, as we are instructed to do in 1 Thessalonians 5:17, "Pray without ceasing" (ESV).

It comforted us to know so many others prayed too. I had read more comments on Greg Jr.'s Facebook that helped bolster my faith. *Got our rally hats in the hope position in the Philippines. Continuing to pray.* Another person wrote from Germany, *What came to me yesterday while praying for Greg was that where we come to the end of our possibilities, that is where God's possibilities start. And that gives me hope! We keep the prayers and love coming.* One of our global workers in Egypt commented, *A group of Egyptian pastors are fasting for your father.* Another global worker in India wrote, *There are little girls in Project Rescue Homes of Hope fasting and praying. They remember meeting the "tall uncle" when he visited . . . . They are crying out to the Lord for him too.*

The #rallyhope post received nationwide attention again when Greg Jr. was featured on CBS News later that day as he discussed his dad's continued life-threatening battle against COVID.

April 7 brought more good news. Greg had tested negative for COVID for the second time. Friends, family, acquaintances, and even strangers who heard the news rejoiced with us virtually. We weren't alone in fervent prayer, and we weren't alone in rejoicing.

The doctors had decided to attempt the tracheostomy on April 8. In the meantime, they would continue to rehabilitate Greg's lungs. Dialysis was a day-by-day decision, and today they'd decided to hold off.

The results of being intubated on a ventilator for three weeks were mind-boggling. This is how Greg Jr. described it on Facebook.

> Three weeks of not walking; not seeing his wife, kids, friends, or loved ones; not uttering a word; not controlling his wakefulness; not chewing food or swallowing a drink; not putting glasses on or hearing aids in; not brushing his teeth, doing devotions, making coffee, praying, going to work, checking email, texting and calling those you love, having breakfast, lunch, dinner . . . .

Greg would have to relearn all of this.

When April 8 arrived, the medical team decided not to do the tracheostomy that day after all. Instead, they hoped to do it sometime that same week. They also decided to put Greg back on dialysis to give the kidneys a break. Greg was responding well to the many antibiotics given to address his remaining infections. We were told these were all good signs.

The reason it's so hard for a patient to move off a ventilator down his throat to a ventilator through a tracheostomy is because there is preparatory protocol for making the transition. This mainly involves trials where they minimize the ventilator settings slowly to see how a patient responds. They measure how he reacts and his ability to not dangerously disrupt breathing, which would certainly affect other organs. It's complex.

It required more patience . . . and more prayer.

Good Friday arrived on April 10 with an influx of emails, calls, and Facebook posts all expressing expectations that Greg would be healed this weekend, or at least we would receive the good news that a tracheostomy had been performed. Our hearts longed for the same. We anticipated this outcome, but would Good Friday be the day the miracle happened?

The trial test continued as they measured Greg's tolerance to breathing on his own. Doctors even mentioned that if he passed this test, there was a chance he wouldn't need a tracheostomy. Now *that* was a positive sign! But the day moved along without a phone call from the doctors. No one at the hospital returned our calls either. All day we clung to the hope that Greg's lungs were finally healing. Any moment, we would hear something.

One thing was certain. A tsunami of prayers was being lifted on Greg's behalf. Did he feel those prayers in some subconscious way—in his soul? Was he praying to be healed? Did he feel anything at all? As the sedation was reduced, were his senses awakening? We prayed Greg would soon be able to answer our questions himself.

The biggest blessing of Good Friday was that Hollie, Jason, and the children moved into my house. What joy! I cherished the gift of family in the same room without social distancing. No gift of gold, silver, or diamonds could compare to the precious gift of hugs and snuggling on the couch with my grandchildren. It's hard to express the psychological effect touch has on a person.

Now my house echoed with the sounds of voices, laughter, and children clowning around.

Together we cooked meals, cleaned the house, prayed, shared Bible verses, had lively discussions on various subjects, divided the rooms for school Zoom calls for all hours of the day, argued over movies and shows, and enjoyed all the normal family drill.

Good Friday came to an end without Greg receiving his miracle, but the weekend wasn't over yet.

We busied ourselves with finalizing meal plans the day before Easter. Whether Greg was here with us or not—whether we had received a miracle or not—Christ's death and resurrection had to be celebrated more than ever. It was the reason for our hope. Greg would have insisted upon it.

During our prepping, Greg Jr. called to let us know Greg had *not* passed the trial test after all. That meant he would need the tracheostomy. The doctors believed it must be done soon, hopefully Monday, April 13. Two more days of waiting.

We were disappointed. Our hopes to avoid the tracheostomy had been dashed. The possibility that a tracheostomy would not be successful loomed over our heads. It seemed there was always one more hurdle to jump. But we hung onto the verses in 1 Thessalonians 5:16–18: "Always be joyful. Never stop praying. Be thankful in all circumstances, for this is God's will for you who belong to Christ Jesus" (NLT).

I had often contemplated this verse. The words *always*, *all*, and *never* were the most puzzling. How can God expect us to be thankful in all circumstances? I have come to understand this verse more as my faith grows. It's absolutely true that He's worthy of our trust.

I love what Paul David Tripp shares in his book, *New Morning Mercies*.

> The more you meditate on His glory, His power, His wisdom, His grace, His faithfulness, His righteousness, His patience, His zeal to redeem, and His commitment to His eternal promises to you, the more you can deal with mystery in your life. Why? Because you know the One behind the mystery is gloriously good, worthy not only of your trust but also the worship of your heart.[2]

So, when He says it is His will for us to *always* be joyful, *never* stop praying, and be thankful in *all* things, I trust Him enough to know that even though I may not understand the mystery of His plans, I can trust that they are always for my good. No matter how they turn out, they will always draw us closer to Him and increase our faith if we will allow it, proving the power of His Word. It doesn't matter how deep the pit we find ourselves in, if we are children of God, He is there with us, working even when we don't feel it or see it. This was never clearer than

---

2   Paul David Tripp, *New Morning Mercies* (Wheaton: Crossway, 2014).

during an Easter weekend trip when our children were very young in 1982.

We had traveled the short distance from Salzburg, Austria, to Graz, Austria, at the invitation of pastors in Graz to join them for a weekend of ministry.

Through the picture window in their farmhouse, we watched our children playing outside. A traditional coffee and cake sat on a perfectly pressed tablecloth, with bone china cups and saucers for Greg and me and our two friends. The Austrians are people of great class and finesse. Afternoon coffee and cake made a person feel like they were visiting royalty. It was a pleasant but chilly spring day in April as I watched seven-year-old Hollie near a tree looking up at its branches. Greg Jr., who was almost five, played nearby.

> "The more you meditate on His glory, His power, His wisdom, His grace, His faithfulness, His righteousness, His patience, His zeal to redeem, and His commitment to His eternal promises to you, the more you can deal with mystery in your life."

Since the children were enjoying themselves, I turned my attention to our host and hostess. While in conversation, I heard a bloodcurdling scream. My head swung around to peer out the window. Something was wrong with Greg Jr.

Greg and I leaped from our chairs, followed closely by our hosts, and raced to the door. As we ran across the yard, different scenarios ran through my mind as to what had happened. Did their dog bite him? Was it a snake? Greg Jr.'s frantic screams continued even as we knelt beside him. We felt up and down his trembling body trying to detect where he was injured. No matter how much we asked, he seemed unable to utter a word and was inconsolable.

My eyes darted around, searching for answers. Where was Hollie? That was when I spotted an uncovered well. I froze.

Greg noticed it at the same time, "Oh no! Hollie must have fallen into the well!"

Shock radiated through me. "Oh, my God, Hollie is dead!" My heart filled with fear and dread.

Greg rushed to look over the rim and saw Hollie's head far below, bobbing just above the water about fifteen feet (5 meters) down as she clung to a rung on the side. She had never learned to swim because of her intense fear of water. How was it that she was still alive?

"Hollie, I'm coming to get you. Don't be afraid." Greg eased himself over the edge and carefully climbed down the rungs that stuck out all around the circumference of the well. He had to lower himself into the water to wrap his arms around our daughter, and then began the arduous climb back up.

Once we had cleaned Hollie and realized she wasn't harmed beyond several scratches and torn clothes, she explained what had happened.

She'd noticed a metal box in the farmyard that would work perfectly as a step to help her climb the tree nearby. When she tried to lift it, it was too heavy. She called out to Greg Jr. to help her, but he didn't want to, so that left her no other option than to manage on her own. She pushed and tried to lift it with all her might, not realizing it was the cover to the well. She continued tugging, and when it suddenly sprung free, Hollie lost her balance and fell over the edge headfirst into the well.

How she managed to fall without hitting her head on the many metal rungs around the inside of the well baffled us.

Hollie explained that the deep well was half full of ice-cold water. She thought she was going to drown, but then she heard a voice whisper in her ear, "Don't be afraid, Hollie. I'm here with you. You're safe in my hands. On the side of the well is a metal rung. Stretch your hand out and you will find it. Hold tightly to it and wait. You can bob your head in and out of the water until your dad comes to get you out of the well. You don't need to be afraid, Hollie." She knew without a doubt it was an angel. She wasn't afraid.

The little girl who had been too scared to learn to swim felt no fear in the depths of the well while submerged in water to her ears.

Amazingly, this incident never caused trauma for Hollie, nor did she have nightmares. Instead, it was a turning point. Hollie finally learned to swim. It also affirmed her faith. From that moment on, she had no difficulty entrusting her entire future into God's care, and she thanked God for the ministry of His angels.

Just like God had watched and cared for Hollie in that dark well all alone, He was also with Greg in his quarantined ICU room. He was breathing new life into Greg's lungs. God had shown it to me in my dream. Daily, I continued to think about that dream, and I didn't waver in my trust that Jesus was healing him. It was just a matter of time. The ups and downs were an attempt to distract us from what God was doing, but we chose instead to continue to pray and thank Him.

Easter was strange in several ways. First, Greg couldn't be with us. After so many years of celebrating together, his absence was daunting. The other thing that was unique this year was that all the churches were closed. Easter services were held online while families sat around their television to worship God and celebrate the resurrection of their Savior. Although I was thankful for our church which had sought new ways to minister without physically meeting together, it couldn't compare to the vibrant fellowship when Christians congregate together in corporate worship.

This day in 2020, no one ate in restaurants, although people could place orders and have them delivered to their cars or homes. Community Easter egg hunts were canceled.

But one thing remained the same in our family. We worshiped God. Jason led in a talk about Easter, and we read Matthew 26–28 together.

We ended the day with a conversation with Greg Jr., Lesley, and the four grandchildren in California. They celebrated Easter with just the six of them. Everyone commented on how weird the day had been, especially since Greg's cheery voice had not been a part of the family chatter. We felt homesick for his presence in our lives.

The tracheostomy scheduled for the next day weighed on our minds. This would allow the medical team to begin to reduce Greg's sedation with the hope he would wake up. Would they be successful this time? We did what we knew worked best in difficult circumstances. We prayed. There was no better way to end Easter 2020.

On Easter Monday, as we scurried around preparing breakfast, Greg Jr. called. "Hey, Mom. Gather the gang and put me on speaker phone. I just got a call from the doctor."

My heart beat a staccato. What did the doctor say? Were they able to do the tracheostomy? Had the procedure been successful? I tried to determine the news by the tone of Greg Jr.'s voice. Sad? Happy? Neutral? Which was it?

Once everyone gathered around my phone, we took a collective breath and waited.

Finally, with a loud and definitely upbeat voice, Greg Jr. said, "Dad got trached!"

"WAKE UP, SLEEPER, RISE
FROM THE DEAD,

AND CHRIST WILL SHINE ON
YOU."

EPHESIANS 5:14

CHAPTER SIX

Wake Up

Barnes-Jewish Hospital
St. Louis, MO
April 14, 2020, afternoon

FLASHING LIGHTS. NOISE. CREATURES looking down at me. Were they human? I tried to move my hands, but my arms were tied down. Completely disoriented, I navigated through a dense fog.

"Can you squeeze my hand?" A voice spoke to me.

What was happening? Why was I tied down? What did they want from me?

"Can you squeeze my hand?"

A strange request, but I obeyed.

"That's great. I'm glad you can hear me."

So tired, I couldn't stay awake. I closed my eyes.

"It's time to wake up." A woman's voice nudged me out of sleep. "Can you tell me your name?"

Why didn't she just let me sleep?

"What's your name?"

"Greg Mundis." I responded, but what had happened to my voice? It hurt to talk.

"Can you tell me your date of birth?"

I answered, hoping she would leave me alone so I could sleep again.

Barnes-Jewish Hospital
St. Louis, MO
April 14, 2020, evening

"Hello? Can you hear me?" A voice called to me.

I worked my way through the fog again.

"Can you tell me your name?" A strange voice spoke to me through some type of head gear.

What was happening? Why was I tied down? What did they want from me?

I struggled to give an answer. My throat was so sore. "Greg Mundis."

"What is your date of birth?"

After I answered, the voice asked, "Mr. Mundis, can you tell me where you are?"

Where was I? No idea at all. I tried to remember, then blurted, "Amman, Jordan." I'd gotten sick there, food poisoning. I went to the hospital.

My eyes felt heavy. Everything was blurry. Giving up, I drifted to sleep again.

Barnes-Jewish Hospital
St. Louis, MO
April 15, 2020, morning

"Good morning. It's time to wake up and open your eyes. I know you can. I need you to tell me your name."

I could see a bit clearer now. She wasn't a creature after all, but she looked like someone from outer space. I said, "Greg Mundis."

"Very good. And what is your date of birth?"

As soon as I answered that question, I knew what the next one would be.

"Can you tell me where you are?"

Yep, that's the one. Was Amman, Jordan, the wrong answer? Where had I gone after Jordan? Probably landed in Paris. My voice was so strained, I barely recognized it. My throat burned.

The space woman stared at me. Was that the wrong answer too? Where did I go after Paris?

"Try harder to remember. Can you tell me where you are?"

Despite my exhaustion, I remembered another location. "Reunion Islands."

She walked away.

My mind felt jumbled. Where am I? What has happened to me? Too tired to talk, my eyes drifted shut.

Springfield, MO
April 16, 2020, afternoon

It was odd that we hadn't heard anything from the doctors or nurses since the tracheostomy had been performed on Greg three days ago. We called and left messages on a continual basis but received no return calls. Had a problem arisen with the tracheostomy?

We understood that ICU COVID patients were on the increase and a significant rise in the death toll had been reported. Even an acquaintance of ours had died this week, causing great sorrow for those who knew and loved him. I grieved for this family's loss and felt helpless to offer comfort. I did the only thing I could—I prayed.

Then I tried to catch up on emails, answer texts, and get to tasks I'd fallen behind on. As the grandkids did their homework, I tried to do mine. Finally, I checked the news for any updates.

CBS News reported, *More than 145,000 people have died worldwide of COVID-19, the flu-like disease caused by the new coronavirus, according to data from Johns Hopkins University. The United States has the highest confirmed death toll, with more than 33,000 fatalities.*[1]

"Oh, God. Please heal Greg and help us to hear from the hospital soon."

My phone rang. It was Greg Jr. Did he have news?

I listened as he informed me that he'd finally spoken to one of Greg's doctors, who said that since his dad had tested

---

1   CBS News. "Coronavirus Updates from April 16, 2020." CBS News, April 17, 2020. https://www.cbsnews.com/live-updates/coronavirus-pandemic-covid-19-latest-news-2020-04-16/.

negative for COVID two times and his tracheostomy had been successful, they transferred him out of COVID ICU and into a regular ICU room. It was far less stressful for the staff to attend to him there.

Weaning Greg off the sedation was still the main challenge. They had already started the process, and Greg followed basic commands to open his eyes and squeeze hands.

The plan was to move him to a chair and begin the basic steps of physical therapy.

I wanted to visualize Greg in a chair. The first time in a month! Now that physical therapy was beginning—although at its earliest stages—it would open doors to his recovery. The tasks he performed started very basic, but even the smallest step in the right direction seemed miraculous to us, and we would celebrate these too.

A few hours after Greg Jr.'s call, my phone rang.

"Hi, Mrs. Mundis. I'm Andrea, your husband's nurse today."

"Oh, hi. Thank you for calling. How's he doing?"

"Well, we're happy he's waking up when we lower the sedation, but he doesn't correctly answer all the questions we ask. We're worried he's experiencing post-sedation delirium."

"Oh . . . which questions is he not answering correctly?"

"I asked if he knows where he's at."

"Well, actually, he couldn't possibly answer that since he was heavily sedated in an induced coma when they brought him by helicopter to St. Louis on March 31. Greg has no idea where he's at. And I'm pretty sure he doesn't know why he's in a hospital. He may need you to explain this to him. So much has transpired in thirty days. The doctors found out he had COVID four days *after* he was intubated."

"Oh, thanks so much for this information. It's crucial that we know this and start telling him why he's here and how he arrived here. However, when we asked if he knows where he is, Mr. Mundis's answers have been peculiar. The first time he said Amman, Jordan, and the next time Paris. The last time we asked him that question, he said Reunion Islands. Well, we know there is no such place as Reunion Islands, so we became concerned. Maybe he's hallucinating."

"Oh, but there is such a place." Our life was unique compared to most, with Greg having traveled to over 95 countries already. "It's an island right off the coast of Mozambique, Africa. He actually traveled to all the places he mentioned in January and February."

"Oh, really?" she said, sounding surprised. "Very interesting. That's certainly helpful and makes a significant difference. I'll be sure to explain to him how he arrived at Barnes-Jewish Hospital and why. Understanding this will probably help him become more oriented. We will try to explain to him about COVID too. The good thing is, he's waking up, which means he's starting to come out of the coma. After thirty days of unconsciousness, he will need time to acclimate to reality."

"We're just so relieved he's finally waking up," I said, "and it looks like he's using his memory already to respond to questions. Thanks for letting him know why his family isn't there. That will be confusing too, I'm sure. By the way, when he wakes up, please make sure you place his eyeglasses on him and put his hearing aids in. Without these necessities, he will feel lost."

How wonderful that Greg was waking up. How amazing that he could remember his last two overseas trips. The details and order surprised me. Did that mean he had no brain damage from the many days on the vent, infections, and loss of oxygen while intubated?

"Yes," the nurse interrupted my thoughts, "we will make certain he has his eyeglasses and hearing aids the next time his eyes open. Thank you, Mrs. Mundis, for this vital information. We will be sure to fill him in on all the details we discussed."

I hoped the hospital staff would stay in touch on a daily basis from here on out. We longed for the chance to finally talk to Greg. Andrea had hinted it might be soon. But she also warned us it would be difficult to understand him because of the tracheostomy, so the conversation would probably be strenuous and uncomfortable.

I started to research about intubated patients to prepare myself for what lay ahead. Obviously, when a ventilator tube is placed down a patient's throat, he can't eat anymore, go to the bathroom, or bathe himself. Sedation is needed to relieve the anxiety, pain, and agitation associated with mechanical ventilation to avoid self-extubation. A patient's strength continually decreases with every day he's intubated. That's why once a patient comes off the ventilator, he can barely grip or squeeze things or lift his head. A patient may have nerve pain and feel as though his body is on fire. Even months after coming off sedation and intubation, the patient might struggle with breathing, brain fog, and excessive tiredness. And some patients cannot return to their jobs. Therapists have to work hard with patients to help them restore strength and mobility so they can regain as much of their former life as possible.

The insurance agent's words at the beginning of this ordeal reassured me that Greg would receive excellent medical and rehabilitative care. But human strength and knowledge is limited, so once again I called out to God to complete the work He had already started in Greg. We were fully aware that the outcome was not positive for patients of Greg's age after such a long intubation. It was imperative that we continue to rally prayer for his recovery.

Barnes-Jewish Hospital
St. Louis, MO
April 17, 2020

I awoke gradually to beeping, dinging, grinding, and shooting. Where was I?

When I opened my eyes, I saw movement from the corner of my eye, but everything continued to be blurry.

"Ah, you're awake. I'm Andrea, your nurse. Here, let me grab your glasses." She placed them on my nose and then helped me with my hearing aid. "Is that better?"

"Yes." What a crazy-sounding voice I had.

Wow, I could see! I looked around and discovered a television high up on the wall. "Why are shooting noises coming from the TV?"

"Oh, we've put Westerns on continuous play while you were asleep for many days."

"How many days?"

"I guess it's been almost three weeks now."

Confused by her answer, I asked, "Can you please turn the TV off?" That shooting had to stop. Of all the irritating sounds in the room, the shooting was the worst.

Now that I could see more clearly, I understood the "creatures" were nurses in hazmat suits. But why did the nurses need such gear?

The nurse took my hand into her gloved ones and began talking. She talked fast. I strained to understand. "St. Louis . . . helicopter . . . bad virus . . . quarantine . . . ."

My ears perked up when she said, ". . . talk to your family—"

I stopped her by moving my hand. "Family? Where are they? Are they safe?" I tried hard to follow what she was saying.

"They're all fine. But remember I told you, because of COVID, no one, not even family, can enter the hospital."

"Why am I here?"

"You're recovering from a bad virus, COVID-19. You still need to be in the hospital."

Did she say I have a virus?

The nurse interrupted my thoughts. "Would you like to talk to your family now?"

My family! "Yes," I croaked. But where did the nurse say my family is? Why did my head feel so cloudy?

"I will call your son and let him know we are ready for a Face-Time call. I found your cellphone, so this will be easy. And talking with your family will be good for you. I'll hold your phone while you talk. There are other nurses here who will take turns holding your phone too."

After dialing, she talked for a bit, then put the phone down. "They will call us back in just a moment."

As promised, my phone rang.

I looked at the small screen, straining to see the faces looking back at me. Was I seeing correctly? Sandie, Hollie, Jason, and their kids were in a box. I also saw Greg Jr., Lesley, and their kids in another box. They all smiled and waved. Why were Hollie and her family in the same box with Sandie? Was I hallucinating? Where were they? That didn't make sense. And why hadn't they come to visit me in the hospital? What had the nurse said? I couldn't stop looking at my family. I wanted them here with me.

"Why aren't you here?" Tears filled my eyes. I blinked them away so I could see my family. These were the faces of the ones I loved so much. If only my head wasn't so foggy and disoriented. Why didn't they answer me?

"Why aren't you here?" I repeated as best as I could. Maybe they didn't hear me. My voice sounded like a monster in a sci-fi.

"Well, Honey, there's a virus that has invaded the world. A pandemic," Sandie said. "It's very contagious. Because of this, no visitors are allowed in hospitals. It's bad, really bad."

"Why are you on the telephone and not here?"

"It's like I said. COVID is a virus that has spread all over the world, even here in the United States. There are many new restrictions, and one of them is, nobody but medical staff are allowed in hospitals."

Tears blurred my vision again. I couldn't see my family clearly. I blinked and blinked again. Different ones in my family took turns explaining where they were and why they were there. They said something about St. Louis just like the nurse had. What about St. Louis? Maybe they could repeat it all again? I wanted to understand, but my eyes felt heavy, and I couldn't stay awake.

"I love you." Tears rolled down my face and more kept coming.

"We love you!" Everyone talked at the same time.

"I love you." I had seen my family, and they were safe.

Springfield, MO
April 17, 2020

Seeing Greg awake for the first time after thirty-one days was a moment I'll never forget. He was lying back on his upraised pillow, barely able to move his head. His neck was bandaged, but we could see where they had placed the tracheostomy, still attached to the ventilator. His feeding tube was in place, and his hands were tied down.

He was much thinner and had a long white beard. We could see other tubes attached to various parts of his upper torso. It took my breath away. So many days not seeing him. I had not taken the time to picture what he might look like when he awoke. Even though the joy was great and indescribable that he actually woke up, the sight of his raw condition brought the seriousness of his situation back to the forefront of my mind.

We were all so excited. The difficulty with understanding him when he spoke with the tracheostomy tube in place was truly strenuous, and we didn't catch every word.

The nurse patiently interpreted most of what he tried to communicate.

Hollie later described our ICU chats with Greg like this.

None of us will ever forget that moment of him opening his eyes and seeing us via the video cameras, because he was still at Barnes. He was not even in Springfield. My brother and his family in California and my mom and us in Springfield all connected via FaceTime. It was crazy. All these nurses in hazmat suits in my dad's ICU room would hold up the phones. These dear angels, these nurses whom I would love to meet someday, these heroes, would hold the phone up so my dad could see. There was rejoicing when he could lift a finger, when he could move his lips, when he could keep his eyes open, when he could begin obeying commands. They would say, "Lift your finger. Move your toe." He was slowly able to do those kinds of things. Those were all huge wins. We would celebrate, like actually celebrate. We would order in or we would have ice cream. We had to find fun ways to celebrate my dad's baby steps, literally baby steps. They felt like huge leaps.

Those wins brought new hope. Even though we could see his confusion, which was obviously frustrating for him, his mind *had* awakened. It was also clear that his mind had been in deep slumber during his days in a coma, and he woke up to a very different world. With broken hearts for his current state, a desire arose within each of us to make his wake-up process as smooth as we could. We purposed in our hearts to answer the same questions over and over until he understood.

The highlight of our first conversation was at the end of our call. Greg blurted out, "I love you!" Albeit tracheostomy-style, his deep-felt words came straight from his heart.

We had made a covenant the day we were married that for the rest of our lives together, we would say those words daily to each other, whether together or separated by miles. We had kept our promise until the night Greg was intubated. So it touched me deeply when he spoke those words. His eyes had drooped from fatigue, but as he strained to look at us on the phone screen, never were those three words spoken with greater sincerity.

Over the next few days, we saw slow but steady recovery. New facial movements, gentle blinking of an eye, even a hint of a smile that we soaked in like rain on parched soil as we conversed with him through FaceTime every single day. He would often ask the nurse if they could call us again. He did this many times throughout the day, but of course that wasn't possible with all the patients they had to care for. There were so many things he simply couldn't grasp yet.

Greg's ability to tolerate the increased weaning of the sedation was a great victory. On April 19, we received news that he was off sedation entirely.

We were ecstatic! Tears rolled down our faces as we shared the news with family, colleagues, friends, and all who followed Greg Jr.'s posts on Facebook. After 34 days of prayer for this miracle, it had happened! The vent trials were over. No more sedation. However, the vent was still in operation, and Greg required intermittent Tylenol®. Was this the start of a new day?

As Hollie had said, we continued to celebrate every win. We found fun ways to celebrate each of Greg's baby steps, since they felt like huge leaps indeed.

More good news came on April 21. Greg's kidneys were back to normal. Another remarkable miracle.

Greg worked daily with physical therapists to help him move his arms and legs, and they helped him to stand for the first time since March 16.

When the hospital staff told me he was breathing twelve hours without the vent, I cried uncontrollably. How long had we waited to hear such news? I thought of the thousands of people who'd responded to us through #rallyhope and promised to pray—literally thousands of people around the world. An army of believers had sacrificed hours of sleep by fasting and interceding, individually and corporately, for Greg's healing.

He still had a long way to go, but look how far he had come already!

Greg Jr.'s post that night expressed well why we felt such gratitude to our Lord and Healer, Jesus Christ.

> I prayed and pleaded to God for so many things that I needed just one more of. Just one more hug, just one more back rub, one more pasta meal, one more morning hearing you make coffee on your way to your devotions, one more time watching you make

your grandkids crack up, one more vacation, one more football game . . . to hear you say "I love you" one more time. Yesterday the first "one more" came to life. Could it be that there will be more than this? We have all wished for "just one more" thing in our life! Today I have been giddy with joy. Knowing my dad is rallying so hard. Seeing the gratitude in his eyes, his weak smile, his gentle whisper, and his greater-than-life personality!

I love you too, Dad.

As we struggled through our personal battle with COVID, I was always aware that in this pandemic, so many others around the world also wrestled with the complications caused by this virus. Even while I prayed for Greg, I never forgot to pray for the needs of others. I thanked God for Ron, our colleague who had also been exposed to the virus at the same time as Greg. Ron had been hospitalized and on oxygen, but he was finally home from the hospital. However, each day brought more disheartening news reports which continued to impress upon me the enormity of what we faced globally.

While the coronavirus's attack multiplied, so did the ingenuity of our workers overseas, where many faced extreme quarantine requirements. Our inboxes were filled with reports of how our AGWM global workers found new ways to minister to people, even in such a challenging time as this.

They provided church services, resources, and other gatherings online while updating their social media sites with encouraging biblical content. They spent countless hours on the phone and online to counsel and pray with families and individuals. Many took the lead in pursuing new avenues to fulfill Christ's command to preach the gospel to everyone, everywhere.

AGWM flooded the internet with messages of Jesus's hope, triumph, and love.

From Spain, one of Europe's hardest-hit nations, AGWM workers of International Church of Barcelona shared about the unforgettable experience of performing a wedding via video chat. They wrote: *Unique times call for unique methods—officiated our first fully online wedding, with their friends and family from all around the world. . . . You truly can't quarantine LOVE!*

Another couple who serves in Slovakia and works among the nation's Roma (Gypsy) population reported that a Roma pastor led online services in a village where a church plant had recently begun. The online service attracted hundreds of viewers. They rejoiced to see several come to the Lord despite the difficulties due to the pandemic.

In a world filled with sadness, frustration, hopelessness, and grief, believers in Jesus have new opportunities to proclaim His power. Prayers abounded for all our colleagues everywhere as they creatively found ways to tell about the hope that can be found in Jesus.

Springfield, MO
April 22, 2020

In the middle of the morning, we got the news from our case manager that Greg would be transferred to a transitional hospital in Springfield that day. What a surprise! I was astonished. I was overjoyed. Another major achievement to celebrate.

I rejoiced over the fact that Greg would soon be back in our hometown, but what was a transitional hospital? I had no idea there was such a facility in Springfield. Our kind insurance agent explained that it's an acute-care hospital specializing in the treatment and rehabilitation of patients who require prolonged care due to complicated medical problems.

Well, Greg certainly fit that category. Thankfully, the next phase of his recovery would take place at a hospital close to us. Even though we couldn't visit him in the room, at least our family would be able to talk and encourage him through his window glass. We could support him and discuss with him the various issues he might encounter in the rehabilitation process to help him mentally prepare for the road ahead.

St. Louis to Springfield
Ambulance
April 22, 2020

Cold . . . so cold. A gust of wind shook my bed. I opened my eyes to see how that was possible.

I wasn't in my room!

Where am I? Did they move me to an airplane?

Wind and rain beat against whatever I was in. I shivered. "Cold. Need blankets." I couldn't stop the shivers that racked my body. My mind was foggy.

Someone placed blankets on me. It didn't help, so I asked for more.

"I'm sorry, Mr. Mundis. There are no more blankets."

I continued to tremble, unable to warm up as we plowed through the blustery wind. When would this torture end?

Springfield, MO
April 22, 2020

When the ambulance pulled up to Select Specialty Hospital in Springfield, Hollie, Jason, and the kids stood with me outside the main entrance, wearing warm coats, rain gear, and our required masks. The wind was so gusty that we snuggled together to not get blown away.

Greg Jr., Lesley, and their children watched on FaceTime while Jason videoed the arrival of the ambulance and our first sight of Greg in person.

It had been thirty-six days since I last saw Greg face-to-face. To finally see him in person on the gurney as the ambulance door opened made me feel giddy. However, reality soon smacked me in the face. As they wheeled Greg out of the ambulance, we called out to him and waved, trying to get his attention to welcome him back to Springfield. His eyes opened slightly a few times, but his face remained expressionless, too sedated to be able to engage with us. This was so difficult.

Greg didn't respond to our exclamations of love and welcome. We weren't even sure he heard us. Since we weren't allowed close to him, not even to hold his hand for a few seconds, it drove home the point that we faced some tough days of rehabilitation. It was discouraging. We cheered each other with the reminder that we'd received a miracle. Greg was still alive, and we would bravely forge ahead into the unknown days before us.

Through prayer, he had come this far already, and through prayer we would trust God to complete the work.

Once Greg was inside the building and the doors closed behind him, we walked several yards in the rain and slush around the hospital to gaze through the window of Greg's room. The glare on the window prevented us from seeing things distinctly, but we saw the room had a ventilator and other machines for patients who were discharged from ICU.

Greg was sound asleep. His full, white, scraggly beard looked misplaced on his very thin face. He'd lost so much weight. His glasses remained perched on his nose, too big for him now. He looked helpless. They had connected him to the ventilator in his new room.

My heart ached with longing to be by his side and hold his hand. But with the death toll rising every day, COVID restrictions remained firmly in place.

That evening, I received an awesome text from my sister, Brenda. Not only did it bring much needed laughter but also hope.

In my dream, I heard Greg singing at the TOP of his lungs, AMAZING GRACE!!!! I am not kidding or exaggerating. It was like he was standing right by my bed and singing at the top of his lungs! I had a little worship service in my bed, in my sleep, while I listened to him sing. In my dream, I was saying to him, "Sing it, Greg. Sing it, sing it louder. I can't believe I hear you singing in your head all the way from Missouri." Naturally, when I woke up, the singing stopped. The singing stopped, but I was in a total state of worship!!

I could envision Greg doing just that. Often in the early morning hours, I would hear him in his office singing worship songs at the top of his lungs as he listened to music through his earbuds. The sound of his praises to God would awaken me and bring a smile to my face most mornings. Time to wake up! Greg was my alarm clock. How he loved to spend morning hours in prayer, reading the Bible and singing.

Now he lay still and weak on his bed. I prayed fervently right there that one day soon I would hear him singing again.

I loved the words of that hymn, "Amazing Grace." It filled me with joy as I realized again the grace that God had extended to Greg and our family through the difficult days we had battled with COVID. Our sisters and brothers-in-law were such a source of strength for me throughout this crisis. Their devotion and diligent prayers did not go unnoticed.

Two days after Greg was admitted to the transitional hospital, Greg Jr. returned to Springfield even though travel was greatly discouraged. He simply had to see his father awake. How wonderful that now he could also be under the same roof with Hollie, Jason, the kids, and me. I missed Lesley and our four grandchildren from San Diego, but soon, perhaps, we could all be together again.

All of us were getting ready to visit Greg at the transitional hospital, including Leo, the dog. This had become a daily ritual—sometimes several times a day. We all gathered what we needed. We arrived carrying picnic chairs and blankets so we could sit in front of Greg's window and talk to him on the phone.

Greg couldn't hold his device, of course, so the medical team tried to rig some solutions so the phone would remain in place, but nothing worked. The problem was, he still couldn't answer it without his fine motor skills returning. So one of us would run to the front of the building, knock on the door, and ask if a nurse could help Greg with his cellphone. Unfortunately, he tended to drop the phone about every fifteen minutes, which forced us to bang on the window and wave to get the nurse's attention way too often. Those patient workers would smile and walk over to assist Greg. Finally, Greg Jr. and Jason went hunting for appropriate gadgets that would attach to his bed and keep the phone from turning or falling. It was one hard search.

> **We looked like homeless people. It was a theater of the absurd.**

Each time we visited Greg, our family brought food and snacks. Hollie's kids arrived with their homework and worked on it while close to their Papa's window.

One of our AGWM colleagues, who had also been on a vent suffering from COVID, lay in the room next door to Greg's. His family would gather at his window too with the same paraphernalia and food. We looked like homeless people. It was a theater of the absurd. But Greg and his neighbor COVID buddy were still alive, and they had both begun to make a comeback. No matter how insane this might appear to others, we didn't care. We had almost lost Greg, and now that he was returning, we wanted to be as close to him as we possibly could.

Most of the things Greg said were inane and didn't make a lot of sense the first five days in the transitional hospital, but he was talking, so we would listen. "I love you," he repeated countless times to each of us. And we in return assured him of our love for him.

"Water." Greg peered at us through the window from where he lay on his back. "I just want Fiji Water."

"He can't have water while the feeding tube is in," Greg Jr. whispered to us under his breath so his dad wouldn't hear. "Crazy to think he hasn't had anything to drink in way over a month."

"I want Fiji Water so bad I could even take a bath in it."

This was comical, of course, but not surprising since he hadn't had a soaking bath in thirty-nine days.

Our family snickered while feeling bad for him at the same time. I thought he must be remembering his exciting days on the Fiji Islands while there for a ministry trip a few years ago. It was so interesting how the mind works as it wakes up.

I tried to reassure him. "Honey, the therapists and nurses are still training your swallowing muscles to wake up, but soon you won't need the feeding tube."

"Greg Jr. and Jason, I have an idea!" Greg spoke into the phone as he looked at his son and son-in-law through the window. "Why don't we create a nonprofit? Why don't we go to Fiji Water executives and tell them, for every bottle they sell, they can donate a percentage as a tax write-off for drilling water wells for needy people in different countries. Jason, you can head up where the wells need to be drilled. And Greg Jr., you will oversee the nonprofit."

Greg sounded so sincere. We tried not to laugh.

It seemed that even during serious times in our life, humor played a role. As I watched my grandchildren chuckle as they listened to Papa expound about Fiji Water, it reminded me of a very special day back on June 12, 1977. It was a Sunday in Springfield, Missouri. Greg and I were youth pastors at a large church. Greg sat on the platform with our lead pastor and other staff members. A special guest had been given fifteen minutes for a testimony. He was the Assemblies of God Superintendent of the Philippine Islands. We all expected him to talk about the Philippines. Instead, with tears in his eyes, he talked about a country he had visited for a few days in Europe on his way to a conference in England. That country was Austria.

When he began to share about Austria's great spiritual need, Greg started to cry profusely. He didn't merely wipe a tear from the corner of his eye. No, he audibly cried and was unable to stop.

The pastor looked at him and must have wondered what was going on.

I was in the audience with my mom beside me, who had arrived from Ohio to be with Hollie during the birth of our second child. I was nine months pregnant, and this was actually my due date.

As the superintendent from the Philippines began to speak, I started to experience strong labor pains. My mom started to count their duration. With every contraction, I moaned, and tears welled up.

I couldn't concentrate and heard nothing the visitor had said. So, as I heard and saw Greg crying profusely on the platform, I wondered if by some miracle Greg felt my pain too!

My mom looked perplexed when I mentioned it. She obviously thought it strange, but perhaps it was some sort of spiritual bonding or miracle that caused Greg to feel the labor pains with me.

As it turned out, immediately after the service ended, we rushed to the hospital.

After they prepped me for delivery, Greg and I had a few minutes alone in the room. I finally asked why he'd been crying so much on the platform.

His face lit up in a huge smile and he announced, "Sandie, we are called to Austria! When the superintendent from the Philippines talked about the spiritual needs in Austria, it felt like an arrow had been shot directly into my heart. I knew immediately that the Lord was calling us there. It was intense and so personal. I couldn't stop crying. The Lord answered our prayers. We can now make plans to apply for a missions appointment to Austria!"

Needless to say, I hadn't expected *that* explanation. My first response was, "Okay . . . but PLEASE . . . let's get this baby out first!"

Later, we laughed at the humor of the Lord and His timing for such a monumental change in our lives. My tears from contractions and Greg's tears in answer to the call of God occurred at exactly the same time.

Two and a half years later, we boarded a plane to Vienna, Austria, and spent eighteen years serving the country of our calling with Hollie and Greg Jr.

Now that Greg was at the transitional hospital, humorous experiences continued daily.

As his brain and mind continued to wake up, he reverted back to the Western TV shows that had been continuously playing in his room at Barnes-Jewish Hospital for two and a half weeks while he lay unconscious. Somehow, parts of the Westerns had penetrated his brain. He would mention rifles and talk like a cowboy.

Looking out at our kids through the hospital window, Greg spoke into his cellphone. "When I git m'self out of here, I'ma gonna git me a big hamburger and the biggest fries ever."

The grandkids slapped hands over their mouths and turned their heads away from the window so Papa wouldn't hear them laughing. In a Facebook post, Greg Jr. had told God he needed one more time to watch his dad make his grandkids crack up. Even in his confused state, Papa entertained his grandchildren, and the rest of the family too.

That night, after everyone went to their bedrooms, I climbed into my bed and decided to check the news app on my phone. I typed *COVID updates, April 24* on the screen and did a search.

The death toll from the coronavirus in the United States passed 50,000, accounting for more than 25% of the COVID-19 deaths globally, according to a tally from Johns Hopkins University. More than 2.7 million COVID-19 cases have been confirmed worldwide, with over 880,000 of them in the U.S.[2]

My sincere prayers continued for the people and families who suffered. Prayer was the only answer in this pandemic that took more lives every day. We had to continue to #rallyhope through prayer for protection from this monster virus.

I'd seen Greg Jr. working on a new Facebook post that evening, so I clicked on his Facebook page and began to read.

He has spent the last 30 hours without the ventilator! WOOHOO!!! What a great accomplishment considering where we were a week ago. His infections have all cleared and his kidneys are healed. Rehab, rehab is now the name of the game.

Can you imagine being emergently intubated before COVID was really a thing, being chemically sedated for 5 weeks, during your medically induced coma you are flown to another city, dialysis is routinely hooked up, a tracheostomy is performed, you are woken up now in a different city, surrounded by healthcare professionals that look like they are from outer space with all the personal protective equipment on, no family around except through a magical phone, being unable to control your arms or legs purposefully, being transported by ambulance to another rehab facility and then you finally "wake up" and see your wife, your daughter and her family who live outside the country,

2   CBS News. "Coronavirus Updates from April 24, 2020." CBS News, April 26, 2020. https://www.cbsnews.com/live-updates/coronavirus-update-covid-19-2020-04-24/.

and your son who lives in San Diego staring at you through the window? Talk about SENSORY OVERLOAD!!!

I placed my phone on the nightstand and rolled to my side. The events of the last few days played out in my mind. Greg always looked so baffled whenever he saw us standing outside his window, poor man. What a confusing world in which he had awakened. All of us, even the grandchildren, explained many times a day about COVID and how he got it. We told Greg how the pandemic had changed the world, including why no one was allowed in hospitals and why the medical staff had to wear hazmat suits. We slowly listed details of the changes over and over again.

Greg became frustrated when he couldn't do the simplest tasks due to a lack of fine motor skills, blaming COVID-19 for his new problems, often asking us through the window if he would ever get better.

Each time we left for a few minutes, he would repeatedly ask with fearful eyes, "Will you come back? I love you all so much."

How difficult it was to see the heartbreak in his eyes. He'd cry, and then we'd all cry together.

But Greg was alive, and every day brought improvement. I longed to have him whole again so we could talk about all these things.

As I lay there, I thanked the Lord for answering the prayers of family, colleagues, friends, and people I didn't even know from around the world. So many had prayed and continued to pray—thousands of prayers, day after day, week after week—for Greg's healing.

I knew complete healing was on the way. I continued to intercede for Greg's total recovery. I remembered the encouraging words in Mark 7:37 where it talks about Jesus healing the deaf man. "People were overwhelmed with amazement, 'He has done everything well . . . He even makes the deaf hear and the mute speak.'"

I remembered my dream again and Ezekiel 37:5: "I will make breath enter you, and you will come to life." Jesus had indeed breathed new life into Greg, and today he was breathing on his own without assistance: a miracle and promise from my dream. And even though rehabilitation would be our next stretching experience, I praised God again for the prayers He'd already answered. At the time of the dream, I felt certain that Greg would heal without a remaining handicap, but the last weeks revealed just how long this journey could take. And many were now asking, "Would the life Greg knew before COVID ever be his again?"

"BE JOYFUL IN HOPE,
PATIENT IN AFFLICTION,
FAITHFUL IN PRAYER."

ROMANS 12:12

CHAPTER SEVEN

Welcome Home

In October 2020, I sat in a large audience and watched Greg as he stood behind the podium and spoke about the death-defying crisis he had recently come through. One by one, he listed each life-threatening and challenging ailment he'd been forced to endure.

- Infection with a deadly virus
- Emergent intubation
- Pulmonary failure
- Blood clots in arms and legs
- Cardiac complications from experimental medications
- Gastrointestinal infection
- Bilateral secondary pneumonia
- Acute respiratory distress syndrome
- Acute kidney failure/dialysis
- Fungemia (infection in the blood)
- Sepsis
- Tracheostomy
- Bed sores
- Post-sedation delirium

His thankfulness for their many prayers was evident to everyone in the room, and many began to raise their hands and voices to give praise to God.

Greg's fine motor skills had returned to normal, and he no longer needed a wheelchair, walker, or even a cane. He had regained thirty-five pounds and his strength had returned.

I watched the audience as my husband told the rest of his story. He was able to articulate exceptionally well with his recovered cognitive skills. The crowd listened with rapt attention to his words. Most had followed Greg's COVID journey through Greg Jr.'s Facebook posts, and could not believe Greg now stood before them, totally healed, only six months later. At certain points in his testimony, the people enthusiastically clapped. Many wiped tears away.

Greg was back to doing what he loved best: sharing about Jesus, his Savior, Baptizer, Deliverer, and Healer. Looking at him today, no one would ever guess that only six months ago, Greg had been vented for thirty-nine days as he fought to stay alive. After completing four months of rehabilitation, Greg was fully recovered and back to work again.

Despite the COVID-19 world we now lived in, life had become more meaningful than it ever had been. The memories of our COVID battle lingered on and will probably stay with us forever. Our desire is to help others who are facing the same types of hopeless situations, pray with them, and point them to Jesus.

My mind wandered to Greg's rehabilitation process and the strength and determination it took to regain his cognitive skills and mobility. Greg was moved by ambulance on April 22 to the transitional hospital in Springfield from Barnes-Jewish Hospital in St. Louis and remained there thirteen days. During that time, he finally came off the ventilator, and had the tracheostomy removed. Once that was done, his speech was no longer strained, and he could converse just as before. He was finally able to breathe without any need for supplemental oxygen.

During those intense days at that hospital, therapists and nurses taught him how to strengthen his muscles that had atrophied from disuse while on the vent. They taught him swallowing exercises to practice. Once Greg passed the swallowing test, the feeding tube was removed, and he could eat and drink again. They taught him to use an assistive device to walk a few steps, sit down in a chair, and return to a standing position. The therapist showed him how to get into bed and then out again on his own. While doing all this, not only was his physical body waking up, but so was his mind, little by little.

I loved how Greg Jr. explained the last week of his dad's stay at the transitional hospital.

Dad does not cease to amaze me. Every time we talk he is more grounded. You can literally see the wheels spinning. As if his mental hands are moving at lightning speed putting together a Ravensburger 1000-piece puzzle of broken memories, sorting his time under sedation from his current reality, filling in time gaps, sorting out different geographic locations . . . and on and on. What strength my father has. Strength he shares with so many survivors of this disease. His days are not complete until his loved ones show up outside his window, bundled up in the cold, walking across swampy grass to share an "in-person" phone call. His gratefulness is often expressed with tears and verbal thanks.

On May 6, Greg had improved enough to move to an in-patient rehabilitation center. For a brief moment in that transfer, Hollie, Jason, my grandchildren, and I, while wearing masks, were allowed to kiss Greg on the top of his head. He was also masked. After fifty days and overcoming death, something as simple as holding his hand and giving him kisses on his head through our masks for the first time was profoundly moving. Tears flowed down Greg's face as he spoke in overwhelmed, soft tones, "Thanks," "Praise God," and "I love you." Each word that fell from his lips warmed our hearts with love and gratitude to see how far he had come in thirteen days.

The same routine for visitations continued at the rehabilitation facility. Only outdoor visits were permitted, so communication had to be done through phones again. His fine motor skills had come alive. Greg could now hold his phone and call us. The grandchildren never grew tired of visiting their papa "window style" day after day, which was surprising when you consider how inconvenient it could have become after a while. Their conversations weren't quite as humorous as at the transitional hospital when Greg was still in his early days after waking up from the coma. Now Greg enjoyed discussing his "homework" assignments with them, which were given to him to cognitively wake up his brain function. The grandchildren enthusiastically baked cookies and treats for him, giving them to an attendant who brought the container of goodies to his room.

It was at this facility that we witnessed the old Greg emerging again. He fought for his independence, regained control of his senses, and battled for his emotional and spiritual well-being. Greg still couldn't use social media or computers, but he often asked if we were conveying his gratitude to his praying "extended family" for all the prayers, cards, and encouragement they faithfully sent to him. He was humbled by such an outpouring of love.

On May 15, Greg's physical therapist asked Hollie and me to join her for a rehab session. Interestingly, we learned that Greg was the *first* COVID patient at this hospital. The therapist wanted us to see firsthand how Greg was progressing with his physical and occupational competencies—walking, getting in and out of cars, navigating steps, hygiene care, strength ability, and much more. They wanted to make sure protocol for safety was in place in our home before releasing him.

> **She had reasonably feared that after weeks of being on the ventilator, her dad might be a "vegetable."**

While at the rehab session, the facility required Hollie and I to wear sterile gowns, masks, and gloves, but that didn't stop us from holding Greg's hands and kissing the top of his head. We were finally in a room with him—in person!

When the session was over, the discharge nurse met with us and said Greg was excelling in all areas of therapy. In about five days, he could go home. That night, we had another reason to celebrate with the family.

In conversation with Hollie that night, she again expressed her overwhelming joy that her dad was doing amazingly well. She had reasonably feared that after weeks of being on the ventilator, her dad might be a "vegetable" and had braced her-self for such an eventuality. Instead, he was on his way back to health, both physically and mentally.

Only two days later, on May 17, I received a call from the re-habilitation facility at about 9:00 a.m.

"Hi, Mrs. Mundis. This is Kathy, the discharge nurse for Mr. Mundis. We met the other day."

"Yes. Hello, Kathy. Good to hear from you." I imagined she called to let me know the exact date of Greg's release.

"I'm calling to let you know that your husband has improved so much these last three days. So, we made the decision this morning to discharge him today at noon." Kathy's chipper voice spoke through the receiver.

"What?" I was both joyful and stunned. I could hardly con-tain my excitement that Greg would be home in just a few hours. "Oh, wow! What a wonderful surprise! We will be there, Kathy! Thanks for such great news."

I hurried into the kitchen and called everyone together. "Guess what? Papa is coming home in three hours!"

And then it hit us all. Our plans to welcome Greg home with his favorite meal of homemade pasta sauce with meatballs and angel hair pasta could not be ready in three hours. Regardless, the welcome home meal was going to be one we would never forget—a major celebration in any case.

The grandchildren had planned to make fancy decorations, but now with only three hours to prepare, they creatively made a beautiful and well-constructed welcome home sign, which we hung outside above the front door. It could be read from the street. Hollie and Jason made a dash to a few stores and picked up Italian cold cuts, fresh Italian bread, vegetables, a few more decorations, and of course, balloons.

While they were gone, the kids and I made cookies—chocolate chip. Papa's favorite!

The large, shiny, silver number "60" hung in the living room, representing the sixty days he had been hospitalized. It was accompanied by balloons and streamers. When Greg saw all of this, he would certainly know we were celebrating his homecoming.

So much love and happiness filled our house. As I watched our grandchildren put forth such earnest effort to make this day as important as Christmas morning, it made all the rushing around worth it.

Time flew by, and soon we piled into two cars and drove to the rehabilitation facility. We watched and waited to see when the doors would open.

"There he is!" The grandkids spotted him first.

A nurse rolled Greg out of the building in his wheelchair. Other nurses and therapists followed them, wanting to wave goodbye to the *first* COVID patient they had ever treated.

Hollie, Jason, the grandkids, and I stood waiting at the veranda entrance with balloons and signs while holding up a cellphone connected through FaceTime to Greg Jr. and his family miles away in San Diego. They wanted to watch their dad and papa leaving the facility. This had been the fourth hospital from the time of Greg's COVID-19 onset to his recovery. Our family cheered, cried, and laughed all at the same time. Even the therapists and nurses who had so diligently cared for him were crying.

The moment our family and friends had hoped and prayed for had finally arrived. Greg was going home. It was a miracle no one wanted to miss.

Greg used a walker to hobble to the house, and Jason helped him up the steps. I love remembering his joy at walking into our home for the first time after sixty days and seeing the decorations the grandkids had created in such a short time. Greg loved everything he saw and savored his homecoming.

Later, he sat in his favorite chair, enjoying a chocolate chip cookie and a small bowl of frozen custard. Everyone kept hugging and kissing him.

He was home. He couldn't stop crying—the reality he had longed for had come to pass. The only people who were missing to make this celebration complete were the San Diego bunch—Greg Jr., Lesley, Emery, Greyson, Lincoln, and Ainslee.

But life was far from returning to normal. We had to modify our home for someone with disabilities. Grab bars were installed in the downstairs bathroom, and grasp handles, a sprayer, and a shower chair were installed in the shower. Throw rugs were removed. We made the necessary changes to our home so Greg could manage on his own much of the time.

He had to attend outpatient therapy three days a week, a minimum of three hours a day. Again, Greg spent hours in physical, occupational, and cognitive therapies. The therapists were skilled at helping executives return to high performance. Every day after his sessions, he would come home, eat lunch, and go directly to bed. Greg needed naps daily. He was still weak and became exhausted easily.

I can't help but smile when I remember the first conversation Hollie and I had with the therapy manager, Amy. She informed us that she had already been praying for Greg even before she met him. She'd heard about this man battling COVID-19 through an acquaintance and had begun praying for him. A while later, Amy saw the clip on the national news about Greg. Her prayers increased. So, when she was given the name Greg Mundis (the facility's *first* COVID patient), she was thrilled that he had made it this far and that she would now be able to participate in helping him regain full function.

Amy was yet another stranger praying for Greg. We'd never met before that day. How awesome God was to guide us to this rehab center where the manager had already been in prayer for Greg. It felt like another hug from God.

Five days after Greg arrived home, Greg Jr. and his family flew to Springfield. The kids wanted to hurry and come as soon as they heard their papa was finally out of all the hospitals. They were excited to spend time with their cousins who they hadn't seen in over a year.

Zoom school was over for the year for the San Diego grandkids, but not for the Israeli crew. Begrudgingly, those four had to find time every day to attend Zoom classes and do homework. This was necessary, of course, but who wants to do schoolwork and miss family fun time together?

I arranged for an Airbnb rental home close to our house where all eight cousins and their parents could house comfortably with one another. I thought it best that Greg slept in his own bed every night and had the safeguards in the bathroom for his protection. But every day we drove to the Airbnb and ate lunch and supper with the family. Jason and Greg Jr. took turns driving Greg to therapy and picking him up again. His afternoon naps remained a necessity.

Those nine days will forever be etched in Greg's mind. He played card games with the grandchildren, showing off how well his cognitive therapy was working. All eight grandkids took turns gathering food for his plate at each meal. The love, kisses, and sweet questions the grandchildren asked him brought both laughter and tears as he experienced the depth of their caring.

The best part was the daily prayer time. Each day, one of the eight grandchildren took a turn to lead in prayer. They prayed for Papa, asking God to continue healing him and thanking God for the miracle that he was alive.

It was heartbreaking when the nine days ended. There were some very sad faces as they waved goodbye. Lesley later commented, "Those days together met our desires for just 'one more' with Dad and Papa—one more hug, one more prayer, one more laugh. Experiencing the 'one more' was extraordinary. It is hard to put words to those joyful moments."

By mid-August, Greg had finished all three therapies with flying colors. He surpassed expectations in his cognitive therapy. He walked without aid by June and was able to drive in July. He still dealt with some brain fog a couple of days a week, and he still had some fatigue that required a nap. But he was essentially back to himself.

The day came to bid farewell to Hollie, Jason, and Ava, Audrey, Alec, and Aris. Four months passed too quickly, but I will be forever grateful for their loving assistance, support, and encouragement in my life and health, and Greg's further recovery. The time we spent together watching movies, cooking, talking around the table, playing games, and the powerful yet simple Bible time were now precious memories to hold onto forever.

Jason shared how grateful they were to have been with us during both the challenging days and the victorious days. How important that the children experienced giving and receiving love. They didn't just *tell* Greg and me how much they loved us, but *showed* it in countless ways.

Hollie nailed it when she wrote later, "I believe our children—because they were with him day in and day out those days of recovery—brought him 'back' and were the key to his ability to join our world again so quickly. Being there in person was extremely powerful and brought true healing."

It was a bittersweet day when Hollie and her family boarded the airplane back to their home over 6,500 miles away. Greg and I were happy our children and grandchildren could return home to resume their lives. But I had grown accustomed to life with them, which had been a rich experience for me, and I would miss all six of them—their voices, their opinions, the lessons they taught me, their liveliness, and the triumphs and heartaches we shared together. I would simply miss everything about them.

In September, Greg and I headed to Barnes-Jewish Hospital for a visit with the ICU pulmonologist. He was the physician who made the life-changing decision to move the ventilator to the trachea.

After obtaining scans and x-rays of Greg's lungs that September day, the doctor reviewed and compared them to images from April when Greg had left Barnes-Jewish Hospital.

The doctor shook his head, a frown on his face. "How is this possible? Unbelievable!"

"What is it?" Greg wondered whether what the doctor saw was something good or bad.

"These don't look like the same lungs. They are incredibly better—shocking!" the pulmonologist said.

"Do you see any sign that he had COVID?" I asked.

"Yes, there is very slight evidence of COVID damage." He looked at Greg. "But at the rate you are healing, I imagine there will be no sign of COVID on any images of your lungs next year. I have never seen such improvement in the lungs of any other patient who was on a ventilator for so many weeks because of COVID-19. It's a miracle."

What solemn moments as we explained to the surgeon that, indeed, it was a miracle. We shared about our Savior who answers prayers and heals.

The pulmonologist quietly listened while we told him that thousands of people had prayed for Greg around the world the entire time of his sickness. His eyes became moist as he heard our explanation for this miracle, which he undeniably saw on the x-rays before his eyes.

On our drive back to Springfield, we worshiped and praised God. Many of the positive things that happened during Greg's recovery could just as easily have been credited to excellent medical treatment and therapy. But the images of the lungs were proof of the miraculous that only God could do. His power produced supernatural results.

> **"I have never seen such improvement in the lungs of any other patient who was on a ventilator for so many weeks because of COVID-19."**

As we continued down the highway toward our home, I pulled out my phone and read a statement to Greg from a nurse practitioner from Nashville, Tennessee, who had recently called me to discuss Greg's recovery. I had never met her in person, but she was very interested in Greg's story. She wrote:

> I have worked on COVID units since the beginning of the pandemic, providing education and emotional support to well over 100 patients during their hospitalization. It was not uncommon for me to lose an average of three to five patients a week due to complications from COVID. Any patient over 60 years old with underlying chronic illness (or without) who was placed on a ventilator rarely survived. It seemed that somewhere around week two, the intubated patient would usually begin to develop life-threatening complications. These either resulted in death or very poor quality of life. All that being said, hearing the testimony of Greg Mundis gave me such renewed faith and hope. The only explanation for his recovery despite so many critical complications is a divine miracle!

Greg grabbed my hand and squeezed it as grateful tears ran down his face.

Sadly, many of our friends had suffered from severe cases of COVID, and some had died. So, what was God's purpose in sparing Greg's life?

During one of my intense conversations with God in prayer while Greg was in a coma, the Lord impressed upon my heart that this whole attack of COVID on Greg's life was not really about Greg, but to build faith, and I should *watch what He would do.*

In the first week of Greg's intubation, one of my sisters had sensed those exact words as she prayed for his healing. Since that time, several people had texted, emailed, called, or spoken to me that God had revealed to them that this battle was not about Greg. It was to proclaim and draw attention to Jesus, the powerful and almighty Savior. I remembered my promise to God to do that very same thing.

This reminded me of a traumatic incident I experienced years ago while in Spain for an All-Europe AGWM global workers conference Greg and I were leading. I arrived a few days early to set everything up.

While going for a walk, I suddenly experienced terrible chest pain. I tried to ignore it, but it wouldn't let up. Unable to take another step, I sat down on a bench. It was impossible to go farther in my condition.

Eventually, a taxi driver stopped. I explained that I couldn't make it back to the hotel on foot. I asked if he would drive me there, and I would get the money for him at the hotel. He saw the condition I was in, waved away the offer of payment, and helped me into the taxi.

Fortunately, a physician was part of the conference and had already arrived. When I described my symptoms, he immediately called for an ambulance to take me to the hospital. It was a hospital with the best reputation for cardiac issues.

After many tests, the results came back that I needed a heart catheterization. They put me in ICU and scheduled the procedure for the next day. The cardiologist told me that whatever he finds during the procedure, he would immediately repair it, even if it necessitated a bypass.

The entire group of 500 attendees at the conference began to fervently pray for me, asking God for a miracle.

While lying in my room in the ICU unit, I started to softly pray and sing to God. I enjoyed a beautiful time of worship all alone in my room despite my discomfort. Nurses and technicians looked strangely at me as they passed by, but I was too consumed with God's presence to give it much attention. I continued singing.

While praising God, I felt a huge burden lift. The Lord spoke into my heart. *Relax in Me. This is not about you. I am using this situation to grow faith in those praying for you and bringing attention to who I am to those who do not know Me.*

Before the catheterization procedure the next morning, Greg and the conference speaker were permitted to enter my pre-surgical room. They told me that my colleagues at the conference were also in prayer at that very moment interceding on my behalf. In fact, the night before, they had passed around a cloth napkin and each attendee prayed over it for my healing. Greg laid that napkin on my chest and the two men prayed a prophetic prayer over me before they left.

I wasn't fully asleep during the procedure, so I could hear the doctors talking to each other. They spoke in Spanish, a language I didn't understand. They kept looking at something and pointing. They seemed upset.

I asked my surgeon, who spoke English, "Is something wrong? What did you find?"

He gazed at me in a perplexed manner and said, "This is not the same heart we had seen on the test results. This heart is perfect, like a twenty-year-old."

What? Really? God had performed the miraculous!

Many times over the following days, Greg and I had the opportunity to share with the cardiologist and nurses about the God of miracles and salvation. The cardiologist said he had heard once that Jesus could heal. He admitted that after forty years in practice, it baffled him because he had never witnessed anything like this.

Whenever God performs a miracle, it is not only about the person receiving it. He does miracles so that more people will hear about Him. In Luke 18:42–43, we read, "Jesus said to him, 'Receive your sight; your faith has healed you.' Immediately he received his sight and followed Jesus, praising God. When all the people saw it, they also praised God."

The Lord performs miracles to increase the faith of believers. Thousands who rallied in prayer for Greg have shared testimonies that their faith was built as they saw the Lord perform a miracle in Greg's broken body. They now had increased faith to pray for others.

Two years later in October of 2022, Greg and I attended the World Assemblies of God Conference in Medellin, Colombia. The night before the conference started, I began to feel sick with a fever, chills, and a horrible sore throat.

As the next few days passed, I knew I was having an asthma flare-up and needed an antibiotic and some special attention. Since we didn't speak Spanish and knew nothing about the hospital system there, we thought the best thing to do would be to contact one of our global workers from Mexico, Sandy, who attended this conference. She was a nurse practitioner and spoke Spanish fluently.

Sandy was happy to help me. She brought along another conference attendee—her friend and a medical doctor from Mexico City. Dr. Erika spoke little English, so Sandy translated.

After a careful examination, Dr. Erika said I had a bronchial infection and needed to stay in bed for the entire week of the conference.

Sandy, Dr. Erika, and I had inspiring conversations during their daily visits to my room to check on me. I didn't realize that Dr. Erika only knew me as Sandie and didn't know my last name. It was during one of my daily check-ups that she realized that Greg Mundis was my husband. That's also when it dawned on her that Greg Mundis was the man she had been praying for who had contracted a deadly case of COVID in 2020.

The realization affected her greatly. She was thrilled to meet this man who had been so sick and almost died from COVID.

She explained that she had heard about him through one of our global workers in Mexico, who pointed her to our son's Facebook posts. She even involved her church in these posts and began a Zoom prayer meeting three times a week to pray for the sick, but especially for this man in Missouri named Greg. Dr. Erika told us they never missed a day of praying for him—a man no one in their church knew personally. When they heard he was finally well and had survived his illness, their hearts filled with joy and they rejoiced as if he had been a part of their church community.

Dr. Erika was so happy to meet Greg in Colombia and see for herself how well he was doing. She asked him some specific medical questions she'd been curious about these last two years. His answers added to her amazement as she stared at the miracle that stood before her. She couldn't wait to return to her church with pictures to prove she had met "the Greg they had prayed for so diligently."

Greg asked Dr. Erika to extend his deepest thanks to the faithful prayer warriors, whom he'd never met, yet they had earnestly prayed for him in their church in the Mexico City area.

Dr. Erika said such news would certainly bring encouragement, increased faith, and elevate confidence to believe for the impossible as the church continues to faithfully pray for the lost, the sick, and those in need.

On the last morning of the conference, the only day I was well enough to attend, Greg was the guest speaker. As he thanked his colleagues, leaders in mission endeavors all over the world, for their faithful prayers, notes, cards, texts, emails, and calls

·during his battle with COVID only two years prior, the entire audience stood and clapped their hands while praising God.

Chills ran through my body as I witnessed again the partnership in prayer evidenced that day. This group numbered over one thousand, and they represented a small amount of the prayer warriors who had rallied for Greg's healing. As I listened to the sound crescendo around the large room as so many voices loudly worshiped with thanksgiving and hands raised to heaven, I fell to my seat, so moved as I heard them give Jesus, our Savior and Healer, the praise He so deserves and so covets from His people.

My heart joined with theirs in worship as I relived the dream in my mind when Jesus had climbed on Greg's hospital bed, covered him with His beautiful white robe, and breathed into his lungs. The words in Ezekiel 37:5 echoed in my mind: "I will make breath enter you, and you will come to life." That is exactly what He had done! God's breath flowed into Greg's damaged lungs and healed them, and his body became whole and healthy. Greg's healing was about the power of Jesus and the power of prayer.

Jesus is worthy of our praise and adoration, not just for a season, but for a lifetime: from generation to generation.

I bowed my head in reverence to Him and joined the choir of voices with my personal expression of everlasting thanks to Jesus Christ, my Lord. The promise I made on March 31, 2020, is my constant pursuit—to proclaim His goodness, His power, and His miraculous nature boldly and clearly as long as I have breath.

"THIS SICKNESS WILL NOT
END IN DEATH.

NO, IT IS FOR GOD'S GLORY
SO THAT GOD'S SON

MAY BE GLORIFIED
THROUGH IT."

JOHN 11:4

Epilogue

Greg's Insights
November 2022

WAKING UP FROM A COMA

PEOPLE HAVE ASKED ME what it felt like to wake up after a medical-ly-induced coma that lasted well over a month. I tell them, my anxiety was over the top, my emotions disheveled, and the environment unfamiliar and alien-like. For many days, I couldn't make sense of what was going on.

I didn't understand that I was fighting a deadly infection. No, *several* deadly infections. I tried to comprehend what was happening, why it was happening, when did it happen, where did it happen, and how did it happen. But my mind stayed trapped in a thick fog.

As I slowly but steadily progressed in regaining full consciousness over days and even weeks, the uncertainty of my whole situation prevailed. I had lost forty-five pounds and my muscles had atrophied. As much as I tried, I couldn't turn over in my bed on my own strength. I knew what to do, but my body refused to respond. My hands were weak and uncontrollable. I couldn't grasp a phone or even press the numbers to call some-one. In addition, I couldn't swallow as a result of being intubat-ed. My throat was parched. I begged for ice cubes to have some-thing cool and wet in my mouth. For some reason, I longed for Fiji Water. I lay there as helpless as a blob.

The emotional side of waking up was a battle—so unbeliev-ably hard. In fact, I had very little control of my emotions. After I tested negative for COVID twice, I couldn't grasp why every-one at the hospital continued to wear protective gear when-ever they entered my room or when they transported me to in-patient rehabilitation. (I had other infections, thus the need for the protective gear.) The joy of seeing my family through the window and hearing them on my phone could change in a moment to feeling lost and alone. I'd cry uncontrollably. I was an emotional basket case for several weeks after I awoke. I felt useless.

At first, of course, I was in a coma and totally unaware of all that had transpired in the world, let alone in my family. But after I awoke and regained a sense of reality, I became over-whelmed by a feeling of isolation. My family couldn't hold my hand, hug me, or even be in the same room with me. The medi-cal personnel wore full-body protective gear. Despite every-one's best efforts to connect with me, I lived in a sterile plastic bubble, entirely separated from any physical contact with the people I loved. I was so alone and yet not alone. It took weeks to understand that Sandie, Hollie, Greg Jr., and their families were each fighting their own battles as my body struggled to overcome the virus.

My family brought headphones at some point in the transitional hospital in an effort to help me feel less isolated. But my coordination was so disjointed, I couldn't even place them on my head and over my ears. My attempt to get them on must have looked comical.

I vacillated between my semi-awake condition and becoming aware of reality. The dream world would cross over to reality and reality would cross over to my dream world. There was no border from one to the other. Everything was real and yet so much was not real. Reality was like a puzzle with pieces spread out on the kitchen table, and I labored to put the pieces in the right place. Sometimes I succeeded and other times I failed and had to start over.

THINGS I WAS SURE ABOUT

Even in this dense fog, there were things I was absolutely sure of.

I was certain of the reality of God and my Savior Jesus Christ. I was completely aware of His goodness, kindness, presence, and great love for me. I was certain of my love for the Word of God. My devotions and morning study of the Bible and the lifelong learning of the Scriptures remained anchored deep in my soul.

It was frustrating to lie in bed and not be able to read or put on headphones to listen to Christian music. I couldn't carry on a conversation for more than a few minutes before I dozed off again. I was incapable of doing anything for myself and was completely dependent on the medical staff for every need. My independence had been torn away from me. All my life I worked hard and had been able to contribute and serve others, but now I couldn't even lift my phone to make a call. Yet in the midst of all that, I remembered Zephaniah 3:17: "The LORD your God is with you, the Mighty Warrior who saves. He will take great delight in you; in his love he will no longer rebuke you, but will rejoice over you with singing." Those words brought incredible comfort to me. God's Word was able to penetrate through the brain fog to reaffirm that I could do nothing to earn God's favor. It was not about what I was able to do, but about my need for God's unlimited grace.

The other thing I was absolutely sure of even in my confused state was my wife, children, and grandchildren's love for me. Seeing them through the hospital window or on Zoom brought amazing joy into my awakening state.

WHY AM I STILL HERE?

As of this writing, it is over two years after the events of 2020. I do not have long COVID (long-term effects of COVID-19). I have no lingering heart, kidney, or lung issues or any other issues. I have testified in person on national TV, on videos, and in writing that I am healthy. All the glory goes to God.

One thing lingers, however, if I am to be completely truthful and transparent.

It's the "why." Why was I so close to death and yet God chose to allow me to live—that is, on this side of heaven? I do know that when I die, I will be with Jesus. So, I live in a win-win situation as a believer in Jesus Christ.

Why was I the exception to so many who could not survive this dreaded pandemic or who continue to suffer from the consequences of the pandemic? Why was I able to step back into my extremely demanding ministry to oversee over 2,600 global workers, a staff of 130 people, a position on the leadership of the Assemblies of God, and the challenge of travel in and out of the USA? Why?

To understand one of the reasons for the *why*, I needed to go back to 2019. It was a very spiritually difficult year. I was under a heavy spiritual attack by the enemy. This battle wore me down and finally came to a spiritual warfare confrontation in Africa, which Sandie described in chapter three of this book. Sandie and I battled for a solid week against the onslaught of the enemy. The confrontation took place mostly at night when we were in our room. We fought so hard in prayer against forces of evil. We read Scriptures, sang hymns, and listened to encouraging songs. Sandie stood by my side in prayer, in support, in intercession, and in loving care. We finally obtained victory through the gracious presence of Jesus.

After our Africa trip, I had to plan for 2019 and the upcoming General Council meetings in Florida in the month of August. The question that weighed on my mind was, should I let my name stand for the election and serve another four-year term? It was also a year where AGWM was invited by our superintendent to have a commissioning service at General Council for our new global workers. Immediately after General Council, we planned a meeting of all our career global workers around the world that could arrange to come to Florida for the first ever conference for a one-time-in-one-place—TOGETHER 19!

After the spiritual battle I'd already faced, I decided to let my name stand and I was re-elected. The commissioning service was incredible as one hundred workers were commissioned to go into all the world and preach the gospel. TOGETHER 19 was an enormous success and proved to be a divinely-ordained event in light of the fact that we were all together, shared in the work, enjoyed extended worship, and experienced a spiritual outpouring only a few months prior to the pandemic that wreaked havoc on the world.

My overseas schedule for 2019 had included trips to Africa, Asia Pacific, and Eurasia. It was jam-packed with preparations and activities. After General Council, I took a trip into Nepal and Bhutan—deep into the Buddhist and Hindu worlds. My previous experience with these religions/philosophies was in Sri Lanka, Thailand, Cambodia, Tibet, and India. All the memories of visiting those countries came back as I traveled in Nepal and Bhutan. Once again, I saw firsthand the desperate lostness of these people. Once again, I was confronted with spiritually dark powers. Once again, I was aware of the bondage of people to systems of religion.

My heart ached as I saw precious people, lovely people, kind people, chained to a life of earning merit to come back to earth once again in reincarnation to continue this unending cycle of reaching for a place of peace. My eyes filled with tears as I heard the endless chanting of madras. My spirit ached as I witnessed young children prostrated before idols, as well as grandparents who could barely walk or stand.

I was broken in my soul as thousands of people circled their temples and spun prayer wheels in an attempt to earn merits for a better reincarnation. I saw people in trances and under the power of the enemy. I melted with pain as I comprehended how lost they were. I wept as I realized that they had almost no opportunity to hear about salvation through Jesus Christ. Even if they did hear, their religion, language, traditions, and culture presented huge barriers to understanding monotheism, sin, redemption, and who Jesus is.

We in Assemblies of God World Missions needed to do more for these people. We had to pray more fervently than ever before. We needed *more* workers, and we needed *more* funds, and this meant we needed *more* awareness of the need. Precious people were lost in a world of circular merit: works, reincarnation, merit, works, reincarnation, etc. They needed hope!

One of the things 2020 and COVID taught my wife, my family, and me was hope. *Hope* is a powerful word. During the year before my illness, God led me to read certain Scriptures every morning in addition to my regular Bible reading. One of the passages is 2 Corinthians 1:8–11.

> We do not want you to be uninformed, brothers and sisters, about the troubles we experienced in the province of Asia. We were under great pressure, far beyond our ability to endure, so that we despaired of life itself. Indeed, we felt we had received the sentence of death. But this happened that we might not rely on ourselves but on God, who raises the dead. He has delivered us from such a deadly peril, and he will deliver us again. On him we have set our hope that he will continue to deliver us, as you help us by your prayers. The many will give thanks on our behalf for the gracious favor granted us in answer to the prayers of many.

On Him we have set our hope. Hope is one of the great themes of Christianity, and its thread can be followed throughout the Bible. Hope is bound in a triad with faith and love, and our family, friends, colleagues, and fellow believers around the globe prayed all three virtues for our family, often basing their prayers on these verses:

- "We boast in the hope of the glory of God. Not only so, but we also glory in our sufferings, because we know that suffering produces perseverance; perseverance, character; and character, hope. And hope does not put us to shame, because God's love has been poured out into our hearts through the Holy Spirit, who has been given to us" (Romans 5:2–5).
- "Be joyful in hope, patient in affliction, faithful in prayer" (Romans 12:12).
- "May the God of hope fill you with all joy and peace as you trust him, so that you may overflow with hope by the power of the Holy Spirit" (Romans 15:13).

Hope fills us with life and energy, enabling us to move forward as we depend on the God who holds our past, present, and future. Fear binds us to the past, creates anxiety in the present, and causes us to worry about the future. But hope releases us from the past, gives us peace in the present, and promises a bright future.

In our darkest moments—when we face suffering, injustice, uncertainty, sickness, or death—hope allows us to keep going. I'm not talking about empty wishes. I'm talking about the kind of steadfast hope that only comes from knowing the God of the universe. Hope is only as secure as the one in whom it is placed. Our family has learned, and continues to learn, to place our hope in God alone.

My incredible executive director staff, Sandie Cross and Bretta Gonsalez, along with our business design staff, created a book of the Facebook journal entries which Greg Jr. posted during my battle with COVID. The cover page has individual pictures of some of the thousands of people who prayed for me with their baseball hats turned backwards in support of #rallyhope.

> **Hope fills us with life and energy, enabling us to move forward as we depend on the God who holds our past, present, and future.**

As I looked at the pictures and read the entries, I realized it was literally a journal of my illness and my family's response, as well as the Assemblies of God and Christian community around the world who rallied in prayer for me and for my family. I was overwhelmed by the support we had received, which caused me to recall and feel convicted about the people in Nepal and Bhutan—Buddhists and Hindus—who had very little hope for the future. Where was their support? Who was crying out to God on their behalf? Our attention to reach them had to be ramped up. It was time to address their spiritual lostness with greater intentionality.

As the summer of 2020 came to a close and my outpatient rehabilitation was over, I reflected on what a trial my family and I had gone through and how hope coupled with prayer, along with love and faith, played such an important role in my complete healing.

My mind again focused on the people of Nepal and Bhutan, and the countries where Hinduism and Buddhism dominated. God reminded me of how I had been burdened for them, and I knew that one of the reasons God spared my life was to mobilize AGWM to work with the regional ministries in Asia Pacific, Eurasia, and Northern Asia to reach Buddhists and Hindus with the gospel and establish the church among them.

Our AGWM mission statement is to *establish the Church among all peoples everywhere by reaching, planting, training, and serving.* I needed to make our USA and worldwide constituencies aware of a tremendous spiritual need in these worlds and give them opportunity to respond.

The "why" was in a large part being answered in my heart and mind as to the reason I survived and continue to thrive. I shared this with our executive committee, and we began to rally around our workers already in these countries and joined them in the effort to reach approximately two billion people who need to hear the message of hope that can be found in Jesus, the Son of God.

Over the past years since the pandemic outbreak, I have lost dear friends. Some to the virus, others to cancer, accidents, and heart attacks. These friends were men and women of God— saints. They left behind spouses, children, family members, and friends. Some were in the prime of life. I have conducted funerals for some of them and attended the funerals of others.

I pinch myself every time and ask once again, why me? Why am I still here?

Somewhere between "it is appointed unto man once to die" and "I am the God that heals you," our sovereign Lord makes the decision for us as to when we enter His glory—heaven—and when we remain on earth to fulfill a purpose He has for our lives.

Why am I here? I'm here to fulfill His purpose. I'm here to do His work. I'm here to finish His personal assignment for me. I'm here to bring Him glory by sharing what God can do. I am here to be a catalyst of hope for the spiritually hopeless around the world. I am here to be an example for those suffering with disease, brokenness, heartache, fear, loneliness, and any other possible circumstance that looks hopeless.

Why am I here? I am here to give hope to everyone who reads this book and hears or sees my testimony. I am here to testify that God answers prayer. So pray, hope, have faith, rest in the love of God who does all things well. He is a *great* God—and a *good* God. Romans 8:28 tells us, "And we know that in all things God works for the good of those who love him, who have been called according to his purpose." God has our ultimate good in His plan. We pray, believe, and hope, and we trust God!

PRAYER MAKES A DIFFERENCE

Maybe you are in the valley of depression. Maybe your health prognosis is dire. Perhaps a family member has died, or you have filed for bankruptcy or are battling an addiction. Maybe you have lost your hope and have wandered from your faith in Jesus. On the other hand, maybe you are successful—with a large bank account, a thriving marriage, and a clean bill of health—but something is missing. When you are alone in the silence, maybe you find yourself asking, *Is this all there is?*

No matter the circumstances of your life at this moment, you can talk to God about it. If you don't know how to pray, consider these wise words from Max Lucado: "Our prayers may be awkward. Our attempts may be feeble. But since the power of prayer is in the One who hears it and not in the one who says it, our prayers do make a difference."[1]

The very act of praying makes a difference in a person's spirit, mind, and body because what we *think* is who we will *be*.

Philippians 4:4–9 is another Scripture passage I read every day during the year before contracting COVID. As I look back, I can see God was preparing me for the physical, mental, emotional, and spiritual battle ahead.

> Rejoice in the Lord always. I will say it again: Rejoice! Let your gentleness be evident to all. The Lord is near. Do not be anxious about anything, but in every situation, by prayer and petition, with thanksgiving, present your requests to God. And the peace of God, which transcends all understanding, will guard your hearts and your minds in Christ Jesus. Finally, brothers and sisters, whatever is true, whatever is noble, whatever is right, whatever is pure, whatever is lovely, whatever is admirable—if anything is excellent or praiseworthy—think about such things. Whatever you have learned or received or heard from me, or seen in me—put it into practice. And the God of peace will be with you.

Throughout this crisis, prayer and God's Word sustained us, gave us hope, and provided the spiritual energy we needed for me to be completely restored to health.

---

1   Lucado, Max. *He Still Moves Stones* (Nashville: Thomas Nelson, 2013), 92.

IN CONCLUSION

I am ready to conclude this book. But first, I want to share several things that are deeply meaningful to me:

1. *God is not finished with me yet.* I don't know the next chapter, but whether it's a continuation of His work in me to the world or if it's a conclusion, I am His.

2. *God uses our stories to bring Him glory.* My story—our story—is exactly that—our story. You have a story too, so share it. It will encourage others to share their stories. And who knows, it could be the catalyst for hope, faith, and love in their lives.

3. *God heals, and He can heal you.* My story is not an isolated case. God has dramatically healed countless people, and His healing power is available to you. Randy Hurst, a dear friend of mine, speaks of the result of prayer as being twofold—either *deliverance* or *endurance*. Jesus *delivered* the deaf, mute, blind, sick, and even raised the dead. However, Jesus himself *endured* the humiliation of being falsely accused, the torture of being flogged by Roman soldiers, the agony of being separated from God, and the pain of wearing a crown of thorns. He was nailed to a cross and hung in a position where He could barely breathe. He endured death itself because He knew that resurrection was around the corner. If you are not delivered in the way you expected, then endure with hope, because disease and suffering will eventually give way to new life if you are a follower of Jesus.

4. *The Lord gives grace to the humble.* The farther on this life journey I go, the more I am humbled by God's grace. People all around the world from all walks of life call, text, and message me to share personal needs or ask me to pray for someone else. I am humbled to have the privilege of honoring God's unwavering plan and purpose for my life. I am humbled by fellow believers who have lost loved ones and endured unbelievable suffering but are still able to rejoice that God has healed *me*. I am humbled by my faithful, unconditionally loving wife. I am humbled by my son's and daughter's commitment to their mother and me through the darkest hours of our battle. I am humbled by my son-in-law's and daughter-in-law's love and unselfish sacrifice. I am humbled by my grandchildren's strong faith in Jesus and their relentless love, care, and prayers for me. Finally, I am humbled by the vast number of extended family, friends, colleagues, and even strangers who prayed for God's healing touch in my life and never gave up hope.

After my granddaughter, Audrey, who was fourteen at that time, returned to her home overseas after having spent four months with us in Springfield, Missouri, she wrote to me for my birthday in October 2020.

> I want to tell you that on the day that you were first put in the hospital was one of the hardest and scariest days of my life. But on that day, I felt more connected to you and God than I ever had in my whole life. Me and Mommy had stayed up all night praying. Around 5 a.m. I fell asleep on the couch. An hour later I saw Mommy answer the phone, and she started to cry. I went on

my knees and started to pray again. I felt God's presence with me. He was telling me that everything would be all right. Of course, it took a very hard and long time for you to be healed, and it was a rough journey, but in the end you were healed, and that taught me to have faith in God.

Thank you for taking the time to read this journey—our story. We pray your faith in Jesus will soar and your hope in Him abound.

Acknowledgments

I AM CONSUMED WITH a deep-seated feeling of thankfulness in my soul. I can hardly describe my depth of gratitude. As I write this, I'm making my way through an entire box of Kleenex. As soon as I wipe away a tear, more follow, and I have to blow my nose. All the while, I thank God over and over again. I have so much to be thankful for.

I'm thankful for God the Father, my Savior Jesus Christ, and the Holy Spirit.

I'm thankful for my wife, Sandie, who never gave up, but faced my impending death and released me into the loving hands of God. She's an incredible spiritual, insightful, and awesome person. As of this date, we have been married fifty-one years and counting. She demonstrated great perseverance through my battle with COVID, her bout with the pandemic, and also in writing this book.

I'm thankful for my children and grandchildren. Words cannot express my depth of gratitude for Hollie, Jason, Ava, Audrey, Alec, and Aris for leaving Israel to come and be with their mom and nonni and with me in my worst condition. Words fail for me to describe the thanks I owe my son. His posts on Facebook journaling my saga grabbed the attention of my brothers and sisters in Christ across the United States and even around the world. In fact, people of different philosophies and religions even prayed for me. I'm thankful for Lesley, my daughter-in-law, who released her husband to come to Springfield in very uncertain times during a pandemic when I was admitted to the hospital with about a ten percent chance to live through the night. This allowed Greg Jr. to be with Sandie and me as much as the restrictions allowed at that time. I'm thankful for my grandkids, Emery, Greyson, Lincoln, and Ainslee, who prayed for me.

I'm thankful for my sisters and brothers-in-law and Sandie's sisters and brothers-in-law who supported Sandie and prayed for me.

I'm thankful for Anneliese Dalaba, our ghostwriter and decades-long friend. Her story of the grace of God in her life, in spite of loss, is worth hearing.

I'm thankful for Randy Hurst, my dear friend since college, for his unending encouragement and support, as well as his eye for detail in the publication of this book.

I'm thankful for the first responders, nurses, nurse's aides, doctors, physician's assistants, and technicians who knowingly put their lives on the line to save me.

I'm thankful for the inpatient and outpatient rehabilitation therapists who worked so hard to help me get back to normal, both physically and mentally. There are so many stories I could share here.

I'm thankful for the Assemblies of God and its leadership who prayed for me and supported me.

I'm deeply grateful for Kevin Donaldson, the administrator of AGWM, and the entire Executive Committee, my friends and colleagues, who carried the work of our mission and prayed for me.

I'm grateful for Colleen Price and her co-workers who were responsible for the transcription from audio dictation to written word.

I'm grateful for my colleague, Liz Hightower, who put together the booklet of Greg Jr.'s posts and did a great service in preserving a historical record of my journey from sickness to health.

My heartfelt thanks to Sandie Cross and Bretta Gonsalez, who serve the executive office as my staff, colleagues, and friends.

Thank you, Carolyn McElroy, for carefully reading and editing large portions of this book.

Thank you, David Welday and your experienced and capable staff at HigherLife Publishing and Marketing for helping us to achieve our publishing goals.

With deepest appreciation,
Greg Mundis